Telling the Stories

American Indian Studies

Elizabeth Hoffman Nelson and Malcolm A. Nelson
General Editors

Vol. 7

PETER LANG
New York • Washington, D.C./Baltimore • Boston • Bern
Frankfurt am Main • Berlin • Brussels • Vienna • Oxford

Telling the Stories

Essays on American Indian Literatures and Cultures

Edited by
Elizabeth Hoffman Nelson
& Malcolm A. Nelson

PETER LANG
New York • Washington, D.C./Baltimore • Boston • Bern
Frankfurt am Main • Berlin • Brussels • Vienna • Oxford

Library of Congress Cataloging-in-Publication Data

Telling the stories: essays on American Indian literatures and cultures /
edited by Elizabeth Hoffman Nelson and Malcolm A. Nelson.
p. cm. — (American Indian studies; vol. 7)
Includes bibliographical references and index.
1. American literature—Indian authors—History and criticism.
2. Storytelling in literature. 3. Indians of North America. 4. Indians in literature.
I. Nelson, Elizabeth Hoffman. II. Nelson, Malcolm A. (Malcolm Anthony).
III. American Culture Association. Meeting (1997: San Antonio, Tex.).
IV. Series: American Indian studies; v. 7.
PS153.I52 T45   810.9'897—dc21   99-30804
ISBN 0-8204-3954-1
ISSN 1058-563X

Die Deutsche Bibliothek-CIP-Einheitsaufnahme

Telling the stories: essays on American Indian literatures and cultures /
ed. by: Elizabeth Hoffman Nelson and Malcolm A. Nelson.
–New York; Washington, D.C./Baltimore; Boston; Bern;
Frankfurt am Main; Berlin; Brussels; Vienna; Oxford: Lang.
(American Indian studies; Vol. 7)
ISBN 0-8204-3954-1

Cover design by Joni Holst

The paper in this book meets the guidelines for permanence and durability
of the Committee on Production Guidelines for Book Longevity
of the Council of Library Resources.

Printed in the United States of America

These stories are dedicated to
Mom and Dad
with love

Contents

Preface

Bill Asikinack (Anishinaabe), a professor at the Saskatchewan Indian Federated College, began his 1996 American Culture Association presentation by wordlessly motioning the audience to put their chairs in a circle. We gladly obliged. Once the circle was formed, Bill closed his eyes, paused and then began to speak—in what I assumed was Anishinaabemowin. As chair of the panel, and the entire "American Indian Literatures and Cultures" area, I was worried. Here were two firsts for this academic conference—the formation of a talking circle and a "paper" delivered in a *very* foreign tongue. Bill continued to talk for several minutes, then looked at me and said something with a questioning inflection. Amidst a roomful of chuckles, I shrugged and answered, "I guess so?" Bill smiled and responded, "Okay then, I guess I will have to speak in a foreign language." And then his "paper," entitled "The Interpretation of Oral Tradition as Seen from One Aboriginal Perspective," began with a story.

●

At the 1997 ACA Conference in San Antonio, Professor John Haddox (Pawnee) from the University of Texas at El Paso, gave a presentation called "Growing Up Pawnee (More or Less): Native Values Lived." John stood before us holding several note cards, but we quickly realized they were superfluous. He began to tell us stories—stories of growing up and becoming an adopted member of the Pawnee Nation. The story with which he concluded his talk was about falling in love. As a young man, John worked one summer on the railroad—long, hot, backbreaking labor. That summer he worked many hours of overtime to save up enough money to buy a beautiful shawl for a lovely young Pawnee woman. John told us that at a Giveaway Dance for the woman's family, he danced around the circle with the other Pawnee and gave her the hard-earned, precious shawl. Smiling shyly, she acknowledged the gift. Later, as the dance continued, he noticed "his girl" giving away "his shawl" to someone else. John was shocked and saddened and angry. Then he saw another person, and another, with the shawl. It was then that John understood—he had made the young woman happy by giving her a gift. But she knew her gift would make several other people even happier, and so on. It was not the gift itself that had value—it was the act of giving. That, however, was not the end of John's "paper." He explained that not everyone in his tribe could afford to give away expensive gifts, so "wishes" were often given away. A person would write a special wish on a piece of paper and that would be the gift. John gave all of us such a gift. He had written out wishes such as "May your life be filled with peace," and gave one wish to each of the members of his panel and the audience. The most delightful part of this giveaway was that John Haddox had written the wishes *before* the presentation—and he had exactly one wish for every person in the room.

●

Eleanor Hadden (Tlingit/Haida/Tsimshian) traveled from Anchorage, Alaska, to Orlando, Florida, to appear at the 1998 ACA Conference. She brought her mother, her father, and her cousin Jeane Breinig (one of the essayists in this book) with her. Before Eleanor presented a paper on tuberculosis experiments on Alaskan Native children in the 1920s, she made a point of acknowledging and introducing her parents (who are tribal elders) and thanking them for accompanying her and Jeane on their trip. Eleanor explained that her parents were there to support her and her cousin, and to make sure that they spoke only what they should and that it be truthful. After Eleanor concluded her paper, her mother came around to every audience member and gave each one some wrapped candies as tokens of the family's gratitude. Eleanor also spoke with her cousin at a Forum on American Indian Identity—what it is, how it is defined, how it changes. Eleanor began her remarks by explaining that in her culture it is not proper to speak about one's self. In tribal ceremonies, a person will first mask him or herself with a sacred mask. Since this mask could not be removed from her land, she asked that her cousin, Jeane, help her don a substitute mask. Jeane helped tie a small rabbit skin apron around Eleanor's waist, and she placed a black shawl emblazoned with her clan symbol around Eleanor's shoulders. These items served as a curtain between Eleanor and her audience, and with them in place, she was free to tell us her story—who she, a Tlingit/Haida/Tsimshian woman, wife, mother, daughter, and scholar, sees herself to be.

•

**You don't have anything if
you don't have the stories.
—Leslie Marmon Silko,** *Ceremony*

•

The essays in this collection were given at the 1997 American Culture Association's meeting in San Antonio, Texas. As Chair of the American Indian Literatures and Cultures area, I was privileged to oversee forty-eight presentations, from which these thirteen were selected. What continually delights me about this annual gathering of people—Natives and non-Natives, professors, graduate students, writers, poets, non-academics—is the interweaving of the academic with Native oral traditions. Many of the presentations given are traditionally academic, while others, like those mentioned earlier, inform through storytelling. The addition of talking circles, various tribal dress, and the use of such Native languages as Anishinaabemowin, Navajo, and Haida has made this "academic" conference something new, something exciting, something valuable.

I have retold only a few of the stories I've heard over the past several years, and, as with all retellings, the stories have changed. I wanted to share some of the spontaneous orality that prevents these storytellers from being included in a book like this. In this collection, some of these fine authors tell their own stories and those of their people. Others take close looks at the stories told by some of this country's finest American Indian and Anglo writers. Attention focuses on languages and oral traditions and how indigenous identities are defined, viewed, and written about. The breadth of these essays is wide—from the arrival of Columbus to the most recent American Indian poetry and fiction.

I have been privileged to hear all these essays, as well as the countless other stories that could not be transcribed here. This is my giveaway to you—may you find some measure of delight in *Telling the Stories*.

Elizabeth Hoffman Nelson

Acknowledgments

Grateful acknowledgment for permission to reprint is made for the following materials:

The Transcribed Tapes of Christine Edenso. Reprinted by permission of the distributor, Sealaska Heritage Foundation, Juneau, Alaska. Excerpts appear in Jeane Breinig's essay.

Sherman Alexie's "Indian Boy Love Song #4"; "Sudden Death"; "Indian Boy Love Song #3"; "November 22, 1983"; "Architecture"; "Translated from the American"; "The Game Between the Jews and the Indians is Tied Going into the Bottom of the Ninth Inning." Reprinted by permission of Hanging Loose Press. The poems (or excerpts) appear in Carrie Etter's essay.

Sidner Larson: "Constituting and Preserving Self Through Writing" from *Captured in the Middle: Tradition and Experience in Contemporary Native American Writing* (U of Washington P, 2000). Reprinted by permission of the University of Washington Press.

Tom Matchie: "Erdrich's 'Scarlet Letter': Literary Continuity in *Tales of Burning Love* (*North Dakota Quarterly*, Fall 1996). Reprinted by permission of *North Dakota Quarterly*.

We want to recognize the contributions of several people, without whose vision and assistance we would not have been able to tell these stories: James McKenzie of the University of North Dakota helped us start the American Indian Literatures and Cultures area within the American Culture Association, and these essays are the fulfillment of his vision; Heidi Burns, Acquisitions Editor at Peter Lang Publishing for her enthusiasm and patience; Doug Carlson, for early editorial suggestions; Andrew Calandro for his indispensable editing assistance; and finally, our savior, Paula C. Weston, without whose technical wizardry there would be no book. Our sincere appreciation to these friends and others we have forgotten.

I

Stories of Identity:
From the Oral to the Written

Mother Tongues and Native Voices:
Linguistic Fantasies in the Age of the Encounter

Scott Manning Stevens

Linguistic Denial

When considering the possible paradigms that could develop within the initial stages of contact between two alien groups, one might focus on the hermeneutic crisis that faced Europeans and Native Americans alike in the Age of the Encounter and the legacy of that crisis in contemporary cultural studies. How were people of utterly alien cultural traditions to understand one another's languages and the greater issues of the value systems, symbology, and ethnic identity encoded therein? Any investigation of these themes must begin with that first recorded moment of encounter between the New and Old Worlds. This may stand in for the "primal scene," if you will, the European encounter with the naked and unexpected alien Other. I choose the term "primal scene" because trauma may be the best way to describe the effects of the Encounter all around. Regardless of what those first recorded Native utterances might have been, Columbus's journals provide us with the now infamous assertion that a group of Natives could be taken back to Spain "so that they can learn to speak" (56). It has long been accepted that this statement should be understood "idiomatically" to express, not so much that the Natives had no language (since they appeared rational), but that they had no "proper" language (Greenblatt 33, n. 5; Todorov 76).

The notion that the Other, whether they be Scythian, Germanic, or Irish does not know how to speak properly often lies behind one society's initial naming of that other. The language of the so-called "primitives" was thus understood to be a sort of sublanguage—something akin to our notion of gibberish.[1] This denial of the presence of a real language is what I see as the first of three paradigmatic stages of linguistic encounter. In the case of the Natives of the Americas, this presumption along with many others, is responsible for producing the cultural catch-all term, savage. Here the naked body of the Native represents a cultural cipher or *tabula rasa*. Whether bestial or childlike, the Natives needed to be taught to speak the languages of a "mature" culture.[2] Columbus assures his sovereigns that this will be to their advantage. The Natives are seen to lack religious beliefs just as surely as they lack a notion of private property and thus cannot be dispossessed of either their land or culture since they have no concept of either.

Linguistic Fantasy

Next, Columbus moves through the islands, renaming them as he goes (what one might call his Adamic moment): "Generally it was my wish to pass no island without taking possession of it. Though having annexed one it might be said that we had annexed all" (Columbus 60). He then inexplicably passes from speculating that the Natives have no language to claiming that he now understands their language. This marks a move into the next paradigmatic stage of encounter which I shall call "linguistic fantasy." This is the fantasy that you understand these newly encountered languages (no matter how foreign) and that the speakers are telling just what you wanted to hear. It seems where linguistic transparency is lacking, "linguistic fantasy" fills the void. Only three days after first contact, Columbus now freely translates what the Natives on the shore are saying: "An old man got into a boat, and all the others, men and women alike, shouted 'Come and see the men who came from the skies; and bring them food and drink'" (58). Failing to understand their language, the Admiral supplies his own meaning—one that happens to point to the Natives' belief in the divine origins of the Europeans.

These first instances of contact put forward two paradigmatic responses to Native American languages and their interpretation—denial and then fantasy. If the Spaniards were to be successful in their quest for gold, they must understand the languages of the inhabitants they encountered. Since failure in this mission would have been unacceptable, Columbus now claims that they do understand these languages. We must then ask ourselves to imagine just what kind of understanding could realistically have existed at this point. For the Spanish there is a hunger for comprehension and they seem predetermined to supply meaning where it was needed—but this could not continue in any useful way for long. The initial phase of this linguistic fantasy merely allowed Columbus to report the good news (in the absence of gold) back to his superiors. "These people have no religion, nor are they idolaters, but very gentle and ignorant of evil, and do not even know how to kill one another.... They are very ready to say prayers that we teach them and to make the sign of the Cross. Hence Your Highnesses must be persuaded to make Christians of them" (cited in Todorov 44). Given their seemingly prelapsarian state, one might ask why such a people needed religion? However, Columbus's conversations with the Natives convince him that they are prepared to convert even as they continue to believe in the divine origins of the Spaniards: "Today, long as they have been with me and despite numerous conversations, they are convinced that I come from the heavens" (Feb. 1493, Letter to Santangle 42). We are brought to a point where the Natives are all good and the Europeans are all gods.

Yet even as Columbus continues to insist on the prelapsarian innocence of the Taino people, he finds it equally necessary to believe that nearby there lurks an inhuman Other whose society is the direct antithesis to this peaceable kingdom. These are the wicked and cannibalistic Caribes whose very existence demands that the Spanish build forts and consider the possibility of enslaving the Caribes if they cannot be civilized. This dichotomy of good Indian/bad Indian becomes a familiar feature in the reports of other European explorers of the period. If initial contact proves peaceful there is always the specter of a hostile and savage people just over the horizon. Such reports tend to speak in terms of "our peaceful Indians" as opposed to their barbarous and cruel neighbors from which the "Good Indians" inevitably needed European protection. This phenomenon was not limited to New Spain. William Wood in his *New England's Prospect* (1630) routinely describes the local Nipmuck people as "our" Indians while to the west lie the evil man-eating Mohawks (75–76). In terms of linguistic fantasy, Massachusetts Bay Colony may have inadvertently supplied us with one of the most potent examples: the seal of the Governor portrayed an Indian, complete with bow and arrow, standing alone with a speech banner drawn emanating from his mouth and on it the words "Come over and help us."[3]

As an ever increasing number of expeditions set out for the Americas, interpreters become an invaluable commodity. Since the primary goal was conquest and the search for gold and other resources as opposed to anything like the cultural conversions to be attempted later, the first interpreters were usually Natives who had been kidnapped from their respective homelands and taught the rudiments of some European language. This usually meant taking them back to Europe, where if they did not die (and the great majority of them did) they would be sent back to act as interpreters and guides. In each case the "bilingual" interpreter is an expedient or tool to be exploited in the business of conquest. All along the Atlantic coasts of North and South America and throughout the Caribbean, Native people were routinely captured and impressed into the service of one European power or another.

These interpreters come to occupy a quasi-mythological place in the discourse of empire. The figure of the interpreter and later the half-breed is recorded as an almost uncanny bi-cultural double. Their loyalty to either world, Old or New, is always in doubt. It seems quite likely that the continuing fascination we have with such figures as La Malinche, Squanto, Pocahontas, and Sacajawea derives from their scandalous indecipherability. Does their participation, no matter how central or marginal, in the progress of conquest and colonization mean that they were complicit in whatever events followed? Or does that seeming complicity tacitly admit to the rectitude of the colonial venture and the cultural superiority of European culture?

Interpreting La Malinche

Even to take the most famous (infamous?) of these examples, La Malinche, one begins to see almost immediately that Doña Marina is such an overdetermined symbol as to evade anything like objective analysis. What cannot be disputed is the central role that she played in the conquest of Mexico. To briefly rehearse her story: Doña Marina, or Mazintlin, as she is known respectively in Spanish and Nahuatl (significantly before she transcends both names to become La Malinche) was a Nahuatl speaker whom the Aztecs had sold into slavery to the Mayans. Upon contact with Cortés, the Mayans gave La Malinche to the Spaniards. Cortés had with him a former castaway named Aguilar, who had learned the Mayan language and was thus able to communicate with La Malinche—just as she could communicate with the Aztecs in their native Nahuatl. At first Cortés had to speak to La Malinche through Aguilar but she quickly learned the basics of Spanish and then could speak to Cortés directly. It is at this point that they became intimate and remained personally and politically joined together throughout the conquest. Communication with the Aztecs would have been impossible without her, as would the alliances made with other Nahuatl-speaking peoples. Thus La Malinche becomes a figure of cultural betrayal and cultural miscegenation simultaneously. As Tzvetan Todorov writes, she is the "incarnation of servile submission to European culture and power" to some, and the "symbol of the cross-breeding of cultures and thus heralds the bi-cultural modern state of Mexico" to others (101).

La Malinche's overdetermination as a cultural symbol makes it very difficult to see her as a real person in remarkable circumstances, but again we must ask how much of our understanding of her role might we attribute to linguistic fantasy? In the several months that she was with the Spanish before the beginning of the conquest, do we really imagine that anyone would have successfully mastered a foreign language and understood the cultural norms and mores behind it? How much of the scenes of complex negotiations in the encounter between Cortés, La Malinche, and Montezuma is fantasy and how much brute force? Las Casas would point out that many of the so-called parleys between the Spanish and the Indians in the first years of conquest were much more basic than was usually reported. He writes that in actual fact they "communicate with a few phrases like 'Gimme bread,' 'Gimme food,' 'Take this, gimme that,' and otherwise carry on with gestures" (Las Casas, *History of the Indies* 241). We should have no doubt that this was often the case. Anyone that speaks a foreign language can easily imagine just a few of the pitfalls that await the non-native speaker.

The fact that La Malinche is a woman and the lover of Cortés adds to her complexity as a cultural symbol. She and other mythologized women such as Pocahontas and Sacajawea become the site of considerable anxiety because of the miscegenistic possibilities that they come to represent. They are the object of the colonizers' desire and next to gold become the most desirable commodity for Cortés's men. Intermarriage was not uncommon throughout the period of the Encounter and was one of the chief means by which European explorers and traders became familiar with Native languages. One clergyman writing in the Jesuit Relations would even seem to lament that clerics do not have the benefit of what he terms "sleeping dictionaries" (cited in Axtell 76).

Shaping Fantasies

As contact turned to conquest and permanent colonization, the paradigms of linguistic encounter began to shift. Fantasy was still a prevalent mode of conceptualizing the Other's language and culture, but one now had to account for the crushing defeats suffered by the Natives. It is in this context that the myth of the noble savage comes into its own. I would argue that unlike the childlike prelapsarian innocence projected on the first peoples to be encountered, some writers of the post-conquest period could now afford to view the Natives as a preternaturally noble, if vanquished, people. In their turn, Las Casas, Montaigne, and Roger Williams would all add to the growing myth of the noble savage. To acknowledge that these men contributed to that myth is not to say they were completely unrealistic or inaccurate on the subject of the Indians, but in each case a fair amount of idealization predominates.

For all Las Casas's earnest sympathy and heartfelt moral outrage at the fate of the Native peoples at the hands of the Spaniards, he is a notoriously poor ethnographer. In fact, while pleading the Indians' case he does not hesitate to homogenize their cultures as he idealizes them. He writes, "And of all the infinite universe of humanity, these people are the most guileless, the most devoid of wickedness and duplicity, the most obedient and faithful to their native masters and to the Spanish Christians whom they serve. They are by nature the most humble, patient, peaceable, holding no grudges, free from embroilments, neither excitable nor quarrelsome. These people are the most devoid of rancors, hatreds or desire for vengeance of any in the world" (Las Casas, *Devastation of the Indies*, 38, cited in Todorov 162). This, as Todorov notes, does not take us much farther than Columbus's early appraisals. Las Casas reads the conquest and destruction of the Indies as a moral text which indicts European culture, but he does not give us any clearer insight into any particular Native culture. It is worth noting that Las Casas had mastered no Native language at the time of his death. The virtues he projects on various peoples are of a literary mold, and he frames them thus: "The Lucayos lived as in the Golden Age, a life of which poets and historians have sung praise" (Todorov 163). This is more appropriate to the Forest of Arden than to ethnography.

Montaigne, on the other hand, has no firsthand experience of the Americas or the Indies. His contact with Native America comes via his meeting with a Brazilian native, who was one among three on display in Rouen, and through the experiences related to him by one of his servants who had lived for some time in the French colony in Brazil. Based on these experiences and reading the works of Gomorra and Léry, Montaigne writes his famous essay "Of Cannibals." I shall not go into this doubtlessly familiar essay except to direct one's attention to the moments in which Montaigne attempts to engage this Brazilian in conversation and question him about life in his homeland. Montaigne claims to be frustrated by his inadequate translator, saying: "I talked a good while with one of them, but I had so bad an interpreter, and who did so ill apprehend my meaning, and who through his foolishnesse was so troubled to conceive my imaginations, that I could not draw great matter from him" (Montaigne 171). This frustration points to a problem with translators; assuming his interpreter was French, it seems the interpreter could not follow complicated ideas in his own language and doubtlessly would be at odds to render them in a Native language so different from his own. We can imagine that this was often the case where interpreters were employed. However, this does not stop Montaigne from having linguistic fantasies of his own. Upon reading a translation of a Native American poem and having heard at least one Native language spoken he says "I am so conversant with Poesie, that I may judge, this invention hath no barbarisme at all in it, but is altogether Anacreontike. Their language is a kinde of pleasant speech, and hath affinitie with the Greeke terminations" (170). Montaigne continues to measure virtue with reference to the classical past and find in the Native a version of Greco-Roman nobility.[4]

Similarly, Roger Williams begins his remarkable *Key into the Language of America* with a note stating, "Other opinions I could number up: under favor I shall present (not mine opinion, but) my observations to the judgment of the wise. First, others (and myself) have conceived some of their words to hold affinity with Hebrew...Yet again I have found a greater affinity of their language for the Greek tongue" (Williams vi–vii). These affinities are part of a common type of linguistic fantasy in which a report from some remote part of the New World records the discovery of a group which inexplicably speaks an Old World language. Hence we get a tribe of Hebrew-speaking Indians in the jungles of Ecuador or Welsh-speaking Indians in northern Canada (Sanders 228, 364).   More importantly, though, Williams's work represents a later stage in the post-conquest early colonial period. It is at this point that full-scale efforts began to be made to learn the languages of conquered peoples. Before, it was enough to have a Native guide and interpreter; but now if the missionaries were to win their souls they must do it in the language of the people.

Linguistic Despair

This marks what I consider to be the last stage in the trajectory of linguistic and cultural encounter. I call it linguistic despair. Just as the fantasies of the conquering nations were projected on as yet barely understood Native languages and the cultures they represented, now a certain despair came with actually learning those languages and confronting the profound linguistic and cultural differences represented therein. As James Axtell points out in his reading of the Jesuit Relations: "It thus appeared to the Jesuits that 'neither the Gospel nor the holy Scripture has been composed for them [the Indians].' Even mundane parables to symbolize the Christian mysteries were nearly untranslatable for lack of vocabulary. 'Their ignorance of the things of the earth,' lamented the worldly priests, 'seem to close for them the way to heaven'" (Axtell 77).[5] The deeper the missionaries went into the language the more profound the differences they encountered.

Without formulating this difference as a purely linguistic phenomenon, the missionaries were still headed toward a formulation not unlike Giambattista Vico's notion that the central factor in Difference is linguistic. He wrote:

There remains however the very great difficulty: How is it that there are as many different vulgar tongues as there are peoples? To solve it, we must here establish this great truth: that, as people have certainly by diversity of climates acquired different natures, from which have sprung many different customs, so from their different natures and customs as many different languages have arisen. (Vico 133, cited in Greenblatt 32)

The key departure here is that, in Vico, differences in custom and human nature produce different language, whereas for the missionaries different languages produce different natures. As James Axtell has pointed out Jesuit missionaries sometimes lamented the lack of abstract words and universals in Indian languages; leading some to conclude that "neither the Gospel nor Holy Scripture has been composed for them" (Axtell 77). It was not only the Jesuits who were anxious about these linguistic differences; both Roger Williams and John Eliot were alarmed at the number of variants in Indian languages for what in English had only one signifier. How could the Bible be translated and the Gospel be preached without fully comprehending the nominative system of an Indian language?[6]

This despair seems to me to have its analog in what has come to be known as the Sapir-Whorf Hypothesis. According to this thesis language constitutes a sort of epistemological prison. As the famed Yale linguist Edward Sapir formulated his notion of the effects of language on culture, he came to see linguistic categories themselves as formative:

Human beings…are very much at the mercy of the particular language which has become the medium of expression for their society…the 'real world' is to a large extent unconsciously built upon the language habits of the group. (cited in O'Grady and Dobrovolsky 184)[7]

Benjamin Whorf, a self-taught linguist, would formulate a similar theory under the influence of Sapir and his circle:

We dissect nature along lines laid down by our native language. The categories and types that we isolate from the world of phenomena we do not find there because they stare every observer in the face; on the contrary, the world is presented in a kaleidoscopic flux of impressions which has to be organized by our minds—this means largely by the linguistic system of our minds. (cited in O'Grady and Dobrovolsky 184)[8]

What this results in is a delimited notion of the possibilities of very different language groups understanding one another at a profound level.

Though the missionaries would not have formulated their linguistic notions in a manner similar to Sapir and Whorf, there was still a nascent belief that the Natives' languages would make it ultimately impossible for them to be converted to Christianity and the norms of European culture. What this in effect demanded was that the Natives cease to speak their own languages if they were to be both civilized and saved. It had long been realized by secular powers that imperialism should extend to language and custom if one were to successfully assimilate the conquered. The English would attempt precisely this policy in Ireland through their efforts against the Gaelic language. In *A View of the State of Ireland* (often attributed to Edmund Spenser) the speaker representing the English perspective claims "For it hath ever been the use of the conqueror, to despise the language of the conquered, and to force him by all means to learn his. So did the Romans always use, inasmuch that there is almost no nation in the world, but it is sprinkled with their language" (Ware 11).[9] This seems to have been the thinking behind the movement in the United States to civilize the Indian by separating Native children from their families and sending them off to boarding schools where they could learn the ways of their conquerors but not their own languages. The notion that we are the products of our languages and that that difference is ultimately undesirable is at the basis of all attempts to exterminate minority languages.

Conclusion

I want to turn now from this notion of linguistic despair back to the conquest of Mexico for a moment and examine briefly the thesis of Tzvetan Todorov in his highly regarded book, *The Conquest of America*. In this account of the conquest of Mexico, Todorov views the events of this momentous cultural clash through the eyes of a semiotician. For Todorov the conflict is primarily seen as a clash of symbologies and epistemological systems in which the Aztecs are foredoomed to failure for what he claims is their inability to "improvise."[10] His argument about the Aztec epistemological system, though clear, seems to point to a familiar notion in which a Native system is seen as static (even if nobly so) and western European culture dynamic (even if duplicitous).

Todorov sees the Aztec ethos always to favor action over words in the quest for honor and so poorly equipped to deal with the Machiavellian diplomacy and strategizing of Cortés. For the Aztecs, according to Todorov, systems of meaning and value are inherited codes from the past—they retain their value precisely by not changing. This is that by now familiar notion that any people who base their moral and epistemological codes on the cycles of nature, as opposed to linear time, remain in a fixed or static system. All events are in a larger way "predicted" in this system by a recurrence of the past. This is why the Aztecs were known to go back and fabricate the prophesies of their downfall after the conquest—for in order to make sense of this strange catastrophe it had to have been predicted (Todorov 84–88). For Todorov this points to an inability to improvise (literally deal with the unforeseen) in the encounter with the Spaniards. Since time and again the Aztecs failed to interpret moves made by the Spanish against them, let alone anticipate them, they would—even though all the odds seemed in their favor—lose to Cortés's apparently superior improvisational skills. This is admittedly a very quick sketch of a much more elegantly drawn argument in Todorov's work, but it explains my core problem with his thesis. My question is, is Todorov's argument not a much more sophisticated version of the same linguistic despair we encountered in the missionaries and later in colonial civic authorities, which saw the Natives of the Americas as trapped within their cultures (perhaps by their languages) and thus unable to participate in Christian salvation or that larger western telos—progress?

Todorov's account is of course sympathetic to the plight of the Native peoples; but just as he criticizes Las Casas for idealizing the Natives, Todorov himself participates in another paradigm—one which is marked by fatalism and doom. We cannot imagine our way out of the situation of the Conquest once we accept his reading of Native America. Even though he writes only about the specifics of the Conquest of Mexico, he entitles the work the *Conquest of America*. This is, he explains, because in the encounter between the Aztecs and the Spaniards he sees the pattern of future conquest. At this point Todorov sounds not unlike Francis Parkman claiming in the mid-nineteenth century as he did that "the Indian is hewn out of rock and so cannot change with the modern world and must perforce pass away." In the end how different is Todorov's position from Parkman's? Doesn't this enact yet another recapitulation to colonialism by reformatting the linguistics of despair in a semiotic mold?

Todorov and those who want a "macro" reading of the Conquest of America must attend to the cultural differences that existed then between the various Native societies (and always will). We should get beyond the Sapir-Whorf thesis in order to look at the complex patterns of cultural and linguistic exchange constantly underway in a living society. Recent work by scholars of Native religions has also tried to dispel the notion that cycle cosmogonies are static and unable to absorb change (Swanson 279–307).

The incorporation of many fields of study and varied forms of investigation in the field of Cultural Studies is a necessary corrective to the dysphasia of encounter. Unless a nuanced and holistic understanding of linquistic difference and cultural change can be formulated, contemporary scholars run the risk of endlessly recapitulating (recycling) old paradigms of encounter in new guises—whether of denial, fantasy, or despair. To become unstuck from our own self-fashioned cycle of response, we must become truly interdisciplinary when examining the results of our studies and the conclusions we draw from them—no matter how narrow or specialized our focus. I wonder if Todorov had been trained as a folklorist and not a semiotician whether he would have ignored that living symbol of Native improvisation and resistance—the trickster?

Notes

1. It is interesting to note the word "gibberish" begins to appear in English in the early sixteenth century—precisely the time of the earliest English encounters with Native America. See *Oxford English Dictionary*.

2. In some cases the dominant culture or linguistic group may continue to refuse to acknowledge Native American languages as proper languages—such is the case for the Quichua language as regarded in certain sectors of Spanish-speaking Ecuadorian society today. I am indebted to Dr. Lori Eshleman of Arizona State University for this observation.

3. For a discussion of this representation within the context of early New England history see Francis Jennings, *The Invasion of America: Indians, Colonialism, and the Cant of Conquest* (New York: Norton, 1976) 229–30.

4. Not everyone was likely to find so much beauty in the sounds produced by various native languages. At the beginning of this century the verbose American historian Edward Eggelston in his book *The Transit of Civilization from England to America in the Seventeenth Century*, wrote: "the general repulsion to the use of aboriginal words was no doubt increased by the polysyllabic prolixity of the agglutinated vocables that gave stateliness to the intervals of utterance with which a savage broke the monotony of his native taciturnity." See Axtell, *The European and the Indian*, 289. Greenblatt also gives an example of such an opinion by Daniel Webster in the early nineteenth century. See Greenblatt, *Learning to Curse*, n.19, 35.

5. The English explorer Thomas Harriot encountered similar difficulties when attempting to relate points of theology to a group of Algonkian priests seemingly anxious to find out more about Christianity. He writes: "Wherein they were not so sure grounded, nor gave such credite to their traditions and stories but through conversing with us they were brought into great doubts of their owne, and no small admiration of ours, with earnest desire in many, to learn more than we had meanes for want of perfect utterance in their language to express." See Thomas Harriot, *A briefe and true report of the New Found Land of Virginia* (1590). (New York: Dover, 1972) 27.

6. Greenblatt refers to this as "the near impossibility of translating concepts like, conversion, Incarnation, or the Trinity into native speech" (23). See also chapter 4 in *Marvelous Possessions*, 86–118.

7. Ironically, one of Whorf's inspirations for his formulation of this theory was based on his notion of tense contrasts in Hopi—this led him to theorize that the Hopi had markedly different attitudes toward time and the future. As O'Grady and Dobrovolsky point out in the above mentioned text, this was apparently based on a misunderstanding of the Hopi language, which does contain such a category. I find this an ironic example of the type of cultural misprision that can go on even at this level of scholarly expertise. See *Contemporary Linguistics* 243.

8. For a recent reappraisal of the Sapir-Whorf Hypothesis, see John A. Lucy, *Language Diversity and Thought* (Cambridge: Cambridge UP, 1992). I am indebted to Elly Van Gelderen of Arizona State University for pointing me in the direction of the Sapir-Whorf Hypothesis early on in this project.

9. As to the debate concerning Edmund Spenser's supposed authorship, see Jean Brink, "Constructing the *View of the Present State of Ireland*," *Spencer Studies XI*, eds. Patrick Cullen and Thomas P. Roche, Jr. (New York: AMS Press, 1994) 203–28.

10. Literary scholars of early modern texts might recognize this theory in another guise, namely Stephen Greenblatt's essay "Invisible Bullets." In this essay Greenblatt develops further his notion of "improvisation" (first articulated in *Renaissance Self-Fashioning*) and argues from Harriot's *A brief and true report of the New Found Land of Virginia* that the English were able to gain an advantage over the Indians by manipulating their culture. This is accomplished partially through English Technology and also their ready ability to improvise when dealing with the other. Recently Mary Fuller has offered a provocative rereading of these sites of supposed cultural and technological in the English literature of the Encounter—her works provide a useful set of qualifiers to Greenblatt's position. See Mary Fuller, *Voyages in Print: English Travel to America, 1576–1624* (Cambridge: Cambridge UP, 1995) 91–103.

Works Cited

Axtell, James. *The European and the Indian.* Oxford: Oxford UP, 1981.

Brink, Jean. "Constructing the *View of the Present State of Ireland.*" *Spenser Studies XI.* Eds. Patrick Cullen and Thomas P. Roche, Jr. New York: AMS Press, 1994.

Columbus, Christopher. *The Four Voyages.* Trans. and ed. Walter Cohen. New York: Penguin Books, 1969.

Fuller, Mary. *Voyages in Print: English Travel to America, 1576–1624.* Cambridge: Cambridge UP, 1995.

Greenblatt, Stephen. *Learning to Curse: Essays in Modern Culture.* New York: Routledge, 1990.

Greenblatt, Stephen. *Marvelous Possessions.* Chicago: U of Chicago P, 1991.

Harriot, Thomas. *A briefe and true report of the New Found Land of Virginia.* New York: Dover, 1972.

Jennings, Francis. *The Invasion of America: Indians, Colonialism, and the Cant of Conquest.* New York: Norton, 1976.

Las Casas, Bartolomé de. *The Devastation of the Indies: A Brief Account.* Trans. Herma Briffault. New York: Seabury Press, 1974.

Las Casas, Bartolomé de. *History of the Indies.* Trans. and ed. Andrée Collard. New York: Harper & Row, 1971.

Lucy, John A. *Language Diversity and Thought*. Cambridge: Cambridge UP, 1992.

Montaigne, Michel de. *The Essays of Montaigne*. Trans. John Florio. New York: The Modern Library, 1933.

O'Grady, William, and Michael Dobrovolsky. *Contemporary Linguistics*. Ed. Mark Aronoff. New York: St. Martin's Press, 1985.

Sanders, Ronald. *Lost Tribes and Promised Lands*. New York: Harper Collins, 1978.

Swanson, Tod D. "Weathered Character: Envy and Response to the Seasons in Native American Traditions." *The Journal of Religious Ethics* 20.2 (1992): 279–307.

Todorov, Tzvetan. *The Conquest of America*. Trans. Richard Howard. New York: Harper & Row, 1984.

Vico, Giambattista. *The New Science*. Trans. Thomas G. Bergin and Max H. Fisch. Ithaca, NY: Cornell UP, 1948.

Ware, James, ed. "A View of the State of Ireland [sic]." 1633. *Ancient Irish Histories*. 2 vols. Port Washington, NY: Kennikat Press, 1970.

Williams, Roger. *A Key into the Language of America*. 1643 facsimile ed. Menston, England: The Scolar Press, 1971.

Wood, William. *New England's Prospect*. Ed. Aldon Vaughan. Amherst, MA: U of Massachusetts P, 1977.

2

Alaskan Haida Narratives: Maintaining Cultural Identity through Subsistence

Jeane C. Breinig

Introduction

In May of 1994, The Alaska Natives Commission published their final report of recommendations made to the Governor of the state of Alaska and to Congress. The Alaska Natives Commission was formed with the express purpose of finding ways to address the economic deprivation and social impairment facing many of the 86,000 Alaskan Natives living in one of the richest states in the Union. The final recommendations "relate directly to the overarching principles of Native self-reliance, self-determination, and the integrity of Native cultures" (Irwin 1).

Within this context, "subsistence" activities were identified as one of the key components of Alaska Native cultural survival. As the commission rightly points out, "the subsistence practices of hunting, fishing, and gathering constitute a direct link between the old and the new" (58). To Alaska Natives, "subsistence is not just a nutritional or economic necessity; it is also cultural and spiritual sustenance on which survival of their cultures depend" (59). The commission also states: "To take away subsistence from Alaska Native people is to deal the final and fatal blow to their survival as a distinct people" (58).

Unfortunately, this is a point many in Alaska do not fully understand. Non-Natives often misinterpret the claim Natives make on Alaska's natural food resources. This claim is taken to be in direct conflict with the over-arching American principle of "equal rights" due all citizens. Before discussing the significance of Alaskan Native "subsistence," and indigenous cultural survival, it is important first to understand the political assault on Native subsistence rights that has been ongoing since the implementation of the Alaska Native Settlement Claims Act (ANSCA) of 1972.

While ANSCA granted Natives control of money and land, the language of the act also extinguished aboriginal land title as well as hunting and fishing rights. The congressional committee responsible for this act recognized the problem, but fully expected "both the Secretary [of the interior] and of the State to take action to protect the subsistence needs of natives" (Senate Report No. 92–581, 1971, 37). This did not occur at that time, but later Congress included provisions for hunting and fishing subsistence in the Alaska National Interest Land Conservation Act (ANILCA) of 1980.

However, the state strongly objected to granting Natives subsistence preference, and as a compromise the rights were given to all eligible rural residents. Yet Congress made clear that its concern was protection of Native subsistence activities, invoking its "constitutional authority over Native affairs and its constitutional authority under the property clause and commerce clause" (quoted in McBeath and Morehouse 112, 113). Nine years later, a group of urban sport hunters brought suit against the state for wrongly discriminating against urban residents. In 1989, the Alaska Supreme Court ruled that the state was in violation of its own constitution, which triggered a federal take-over of hunting and fishing regulation within the 60% of Alaskan lands owned by the federal government. To date, no satisfactory resolution has been implemented, and how the state should resolve this problem remains a topic of heated debate within the legislature. As the Alaska Native Commission has pointed out, the relationship between "subsistence," "spirituality," and "cultural survival" is a hazy concept for some to grasp (59), yet it is crucial to understand if the state and federal governments are sincere about improving the lives of Alaskan Natives and supporting Alaska Native cultural survival. This relationship becomes more clear when examining a selection of narratives of a specific group of Alaskan Native people—the Haida of the southern Southeastern Alaskan panhandle.

Alaskan Haida History

The Haida are indigenous to the Queen Charlotte Islands off the mainland coast of British Columbia, Canada and southern Southeastern Alaska. Prior to European contact, the Alaskan Haida established at least five villages in the southern end of islands of the Southeast Alaska panhandle. Due to the extensive population losses suffered by Native peoples, the influx of non-Natives into the area, the changing economy of the region, and missionary influence, only two villages still exist today. With the introduction of commercial fishing, the establishment of salmon salteries and canneries, and the discovery of precious metals, such as copper and gold, the Haida, as well as other Alaskan Natives became increasingly enmeshed in the prevailing wage economies from the 1900s forward.

During this era, there was both strong pressure to assimilate and recognition by many Natives of the need to acquire the skills necessary to negotiate within and adapt to a changing world. The time between the early 1900s and the 1970s the Alaskan Haida were undergoing a time of rapid change—a time of both adaptation and resistance to Western expansion.

It was within this political and historical context that the first Alaskan Haida texts (written both in Haida and English) emerged as a larger project to document and perpetuate the Haida language and cultural values through writing. While many of the texts were developed primarily to assist in teaching the language within Haida communities, a few were created with the dual focus of creating a record for future descendants and educating non-Natives about Haida cultural values. One particular text, *The Transcribed Tapes of Christine Edenso*, stands as especially noteworthy in the ongoing debates surrounding Native subsistence rights, because it clearly suggests the relationship between subsistence activities, spirituality, and cultural survival.[1]

Native Identity and *The Transcribed Tapes of Christine Edenso*

Many of Christine Edenso's transcribed and translated narratives focus on the special foods unique to Southeast Alaska and the Northwest Coast, the techniques once used to preserve them, and the innovations developed in modern times. "There is no Native home without some sort of Indian food," says Edenso (13), pointing to the significance of gathering, eating, and sharing the food to Native peoples as well as highlighting her perception of Indian food as a crucial aspect of Native identity. While Edenso often employs the past tense, a feature of explaining how the Haida used to do things, it needs to be kept in mind that these kinds of food gathering activities still go on in the villages and towns of Southeast Alaska, and urban Natives who no longer live in the area must rely on relations and/or friends to share with them these special foods. This is an aspect of cultural continuity that can be maintained as long as the land remains; that is, as long as the land is treated with respect and care and its resources are not wasted, depleted, or overdeveloped. Unfortunately, with increasing pressure from commercial and sports fishing industries, the once abundant seafoods have begun to diminish.

Edenso's narrative highlights the significance of food gathering and reveals an important relationship between the people and the land. She tells of fish eggs, seaweed, fish, and fresh berries. "[E]verybody used to move to Craig, or Fishegg Island which they called *K'aaw Sltaay* in Haida. They used to go up there and gather herring eggs" (26). Although many areas have been severely depleted by the pressure of commercial herring roe fishing, this herring roe spawn is still eagerly awaited by Southeast Alaskan Natives who cherish this flavorful and crunchy delicacy. In the past, eggs were salted and dried for future use; nowadays the freezer serves the same purpose. However, Haida elders now worry about the consequences of commercial herring roe fishing upon the herring roe supply: "If people don't start fishing with nets around here [Hydaburg] we'll have fish eggs for the rest of our days" (Morrison).

Edenso also tells of special black seaweed: "Seaweed was put up in different forms after it was picked from the beaches and taken home to dry ...you either twisted it and dryed it up into shape, or pressed it out in square blocks with berry leaves" (12). A special seaweed grows on the craggy rocks of Southeast Alaska in certain locations. In order to be harvested, the seaweed must be of a certain length (generally, it is long enough in May), the tide needs to be low, and one needs to know the appropriate locations where it grows. While seaweed has not begun to be commercially harvested, some have noted recently that the growth seemed much less than in years past, perhaps an indication of the changing environmental conditions.

Throughout the narrative Edenso stresses the way the people utilized the natural resources of the environment making do with what is at hand

and at the same time innovating as necessary: "…a lot of people rejected that kind [of seaweed]. She made it…a really edible seaweed by flavoring it and curing it" (13). In another place Edenso notes: "[M]y friend…used to say, "Let's not pick the berries in any old way. Let's pick them right and leave some for the next generation" (42).

Edenso also stresses how every part of the fish can be put to use—the eggs, the head, the tails, the bones: "Nothing was wasted. They took the eggs …they made *tsak'adaang* or Indian cheese…" (10–11). Fish is still an important staple of Southeast Alaskan Native peoples' diets.

Edenso also speaks of the abundance of a variety of berries:

> In July, the salmon berries ripen… .Then the thimble berries… .Then…the light blueberries and the dark blueberries… .Then we get the huckleberry…[and] the… black and gray currants. They grow on tall bush currants along the creeks. (16–17)

The reverent remembrance of berries invoked in the order of their ripeness, their colors, and the kinds of bushes upon which they grow suggests the close relationship between the people and the land; time measured in terms of food-gathering seasons. Edenso's narratives reveal an attitude of respect and reverence, an attitude that suggests a spiritual appreciation of the land and the sea; Edenso's narratives also suggest the importance of food-gathering activities to maintaining and perpetuating Haida/Native cultural identity.

Embedded in Edenso's narrative is a clan story that well illustrates Alaska Native people's relationship to the surrounding landscapes as it is revealed in the following excerpts.

> [T]he people left the small village where they were camping in this bay . . . [T]hey sighted a wild man [called] *gaugiit* in Haida…a person that has gone wild and is loose in the woods.
>
> Everyone was paddling there in the big canoe…. Everyone was excited…. The bow helmsman called up to the wildman and asked him, "Where are you going? Why are you going up towards the old village and going on into the bay?"
>
> …And they said, "where are you going and what do you intend to do?"
>
> The [*gaugiit*] called back and said, "I'm going to *Ja'aca* and I'm going to eat some *K'wa.aas* there." *K'wa.aas* are fish that have been in the creek for a while which have aged. They are very delicious….
>
> [So they followed him] to the stream and wonderous different things began to take place. (20–21)

As the people are led farther and farther up the creek, the way opens "mysteriously" (21) in front of them as they struggle to keep up with the *gaugiit*. The creature leads them to a sockeye stream that empties into a lake. Generally, the *gaugiit* is considered to be an evil, elusive, half-human, half-land otter creature (Cogo 12). In this story however, the *gaugiit* leads the people to a highly valued food supply, one they did not know existed until led there. Edenso's narrative continues:

> He was walking really fast. The wild man was evidently headed for a sockeye stream that emptied into the lake.... They relished the flesh of these fish even though they were old fish... .
>
> Since it was the wild man that was taking the lead...the people called this place *Gwa'aca*. That was the name that was given to this place. *Gwa'aca* has lots of meanings concerning fish and the season of the year in which that kind of fish is taken.
>
> ...[T]he people who were dealing with this wild man were evidently the Dog Salmon people who lived there.... . Some of our people are buried in the vicinity, and belonged to the tribe in later years. It belonged to the Dog Salmon tribe and that is the reason why this is our story. This is our story as it was told to us and handed down, concerning this wild man. (21)

The narrative illustrates how an important clan-owned sockeye stream was acquired with the assistance of a spirit-creature—one normally associated with negative forces. Yet the people follow him and learn of a food source that can feed them in the winter months when some fish stay under the ice. Edenso reveals an important relationship between "food" and "spirits," i.e., the close relationship between humans, spirits, and the landscape and waterways upon which food gathering takes place. In another place in the narrative Edenso also tells of a time when the land begins to be encroached upon by non-Natives moving into the vast, seemingly unsettled and unused territory of Alaska:

> As time went on, the encroachment of the many white people who came into the district began to see times when those white people started to burn up those little smokehouses while the owners were not around. So when the people would go there in the fall, they would find nothing but black charred ashes where their smokehouses used to be. That happened many many times to the people. Vandalism became rampant. (37)

The people camped at the food gathering areas, caught fish and smoked them, and later returned to the villages trusting the smokehouse would be undisturbed until the following season. But the non-Natives who came to Alaska had a different conception of land use. The concept of individually owned private property in Western terms is different from the Native idea of land use. Although Edenso does not give details, one might surmise (generously) that the people who destroyed the smokehouses may have believed them to be abandoned, burned them, and claimed the surrounding area for themselves, or (not so generously) they knew the smokehouses belonged "only" to Natives, and therefore destroyed them purposely. However, as Edenso also points out, there was "no use reporting anything to the authorities. The Indians simply did not have any rights at that time" (37). Instead, "to make it safer for the people's food, they started to put their smoke houses closer to the villages so they could watch them" (37).

Conclusion

Similarly today, the conflict over land use in Alaska continues on; most recently in the ongoing political battles over sport, commercial, and subsistence activities. However, Haida and other Alaska Native narratives such as these can remind people not only of the historical claim Natives have to the natural resources of Alaska, but also to the moral and spiritual value the landscape and waterways hold for Native peoples and their cultures. This is not to say that non-Natives cannot and have not also developed a moral responsibility towards conserving the earth's resources, as evidenced by the environmental movement, or that Natives have not also been responsible for aspects of the earth's degradation, given the economics of living in an increasingly industrialized world. Rather, these narratives suggest that an important aspect of cultural survival is dependent upon maintaining this important tie between the old and the new—in which "subsistence," or food gathering plays a crucial role.

Notes

1. Although I refer to Christine Edenso as "Haida," in truth she was matrilineally Tlingit. Her father was Haida, and Edenso was trilingual, speaking fluent Tlingit, English, and Haida. In my dissertation, *Re-Contextualizing Haida Narrative*, I discuss the significance of her tribal identities in relationship to subsistence and other related Alaskan Native activities.

Works Cited

Breinig, Jeane C. *Re-Contextualizing Haida Narrative.* Diss. U Washington P, 1995.

Cogo, Robert, and Nora Cogo. *Remembering the Past: Haida History and Culture.* Anchorage: U of Alaska Materials Development, 1983.

Edenso, Christine. *The Transcribed Tapes of Christine Edenso.* Anchorage: U of Alaska Materials Development, c. 1983.

Irwin, Michael, ed. *Alaska Natives Commission.* Vol. I. Anchorage: Joint Federal-State Commission on Policies and Programs Affecting Alaska Natives, 1994.

McBeath, Gerald, and Thomas A. Morehouse. *Alaska Politics and Government.* Lincoln: U of Nebraska P, 1994.

Morrison, Woodrow. *Xadas.* [Video] Produced by B. Bear. Juneau: Alaska Department of Education, 1982.

United States Congress. Alaska Native Claims Settlement Act (ANCSA), 17 December 1971.

United States Senate. Alaska National Interest Land Conservation Act (ANILCA). PL 96–487, 2 December 1981.

3

The Act of Storytelling and Gender Dynamics in "Kaweshawa": A Study of the *Watunna*, the Makiritare Creation Myth

Heatherly Brooke Bucher

Introduction

The Makiritare people have an oral creation history that records the history of the tribe and its interaction with other peoples from the creation of the world up to contact with European crusaders and missionaries. The creators of this oral history live on the northern bank of the Upper Orinoco River in Venezuela. They speak the language So'to, meaning "people," "man" or "human being." So'to is also the name they use to refer to themselves. Their oral history, called the *Watunna*, is the story of the "Old People" or heavenly ancestors, who serve as models for Makiritare behavior. The *Watunna* is also the tribal record of their history, religion, social structure, and interaction with other tribes and peoples.

The *Watunna* exists in two forms: a sacred and a secular, or profane. The sacred *Watunna* is kept by the Masters, elders of the tribe, and passed on through a ritualized rendition to the male members of the tribe. This form is governed by strict ritualistic rules and is relayed in a strange language very different from everyday speech, relying on semantic tricks, archaic words, complicated ritual endings, onomatopoeias, whistles, jungle and water sounds, and animal movements. In addition, there is an exclusively female portion of this ritualistic telling, celebrated at the first yuca[1] planting. The sacred *Watunna* is, therefore, static—much like written texts. In contrast, the secular *Watunna* belongs to everyone regardless of sex or age and is told daily outside the ritual dance circle. It is related in everyday language as a profane reflection of the sacred. This popular version is not governed by strict rules, subjecting it to personal interpretation and the teller's level of knowledge and memory. The secular *Watunna* can be divided into eight main categories of tales, although the Makiritare never sit down and tell the entire secular *Watunna* at one time, nor in any particular order. Rather, the history is used to bolster everyday activities and pass on instruction regarding social norms. As Marc de Civrieux notes in *Watunna: An Orinoco Creation Cycle*, "It is hard to pass a day among the Makiritare without hearing a tale or at least some isolated fragment of a story as it relates to the circumstances at hand" (17).

Consequently, the secular *Watunna*—unlike the sacred and written text—is dynamic and fluid. The teller can be either male or female, choosing to shape the story as suited to the situation and his or her own ability.

Development of the *Watunna*

Before we can discuss the dynamics of storytelling in the Makiritare culture, we should explore how the history was recorded and translated into English, as this process gives us valuable insight into Makiritare storytelling practices as well as social interaction. The *Watunna* text we have in English is a remarkable collaboration between Marc de Civrieux, a French paleontologist, and David Guss, a Mellon Fellow at Harvard. De Civrieux did many years of ethnographic work in the Orinoco River area and spent much time with the Makiritare tribe, learning their language and culture. Guss spent three years with De Civrieux and the Makiritare, collaborating on the English text. In a unique effort to translate an oral history, the pair of researchers listened to the Makiritare of all ages, as they told them parts of the *Watunna*. After collecting the stories, they arranged them and set them down in writing. Then, they retold the stories to the Makiritare, who were able to then correct the teller, as de Civrieux records, "Surprised and delighted, they gathered around to listen, correcting and adding new details as they were needed" (vii). Finally, Guss translated the tales to English. While the written *Watunna* then has collective tribal approval, it is a corporate approval, not individual. Yet the tales themselves are told by individuals, subject to each teller's memory, talent, and desires. As I mentioned earlier, the profane *Watunna* is shared by both male and female tellers of all ages.

Theories of Storytelling

As I consider the relationship between teller and listener, I am struck by two theories of literature that share no cultural, demographic or genre ties, yet discuss in a similar fashion the acts of creating or telling stories, reading or listening to stories, and the power of the story itself. The first theory focuses on the dynamics of storytelling, particularly in the Native American cultures. As Leslie Marmon Silko explains, to most Native American cultures storytelling is vital to the community; the tales construct an identity, telling the people who they are (50). In addition, Silko points out the importance of the audience as well as the "yet unborn" and "those from the past" in storytelling (58–59). The teller draws out the story from the listeners and the tale allows all people, both past, present and future, to be together (50, 59). According to Silko and other critics of Native American literature, the tale is active, coming from the author as well as listener, while also going beyond both to join those from the past and future of the tribe. The story displays a power of its own, a life that is born through the act of telling and receiving, but then continues on past this act.

Maurice Blanchot, a French critic of consciousness and analyst of literature far removed from Native American culture, explores a second theory, one of the relationships between author (or teller, in our case), text and reader (or listener). Much of what Blanchot says is directed to the austere, surreal struggles of authors like Franz Kafka and Stéphane Mallarmé; however, the heart of his perception of literature translates to any relationship among teller, tale, and listener and is useful in examining our oral history tale. Blanchot sees writing as a struggle because the writer attempts to capture an event, a temporal happening or experience, through the domain of words. Blanchot introduces the concept of the Work, an existential reality removed from the tangible text. The Work is not the text or book that exists on an ordinary, material level. The Work is the being that results from the space between writer and reader and stems from the text. "The writer writes a book, but the book is not yet the work. The work is only a work when there is pronounced by it, in the violence of a beginning which is all its own, the word *being*, an event which happens when the work is the intimacy of someone who writes it and someone who reads it" ("Essential Solitude" 22–23).

For Blanchot, the Work only exists in the space between writer and reader. The reader is a re-creator, another contributor to the Work. Blanchot never dealt with oral literary traditions, focusing entirely upon written texts, but I suggest that the act of oral storytelling may solve part of this conundrum of the author unable to reach the Work, in that through the act of telling the story to the listener, the tale reaches out, becomes the Work for that brief telling, swirls around both author and receiver and brings in all others. Admittedly, the Work only exists for the span of telling and receiving, and this perhaps explains the birth of oral history, the need to retell the stories to capture that moment again and again.

With this underpinning of Native American emphasis on participatory creation of a living story and Blanchot's focus on the author-text-reader relationship, we can examine the gender relations inside the text and then metatextually in the act of storytelling a little closer.

"Kaweshawa," a Tale of Relationships

Within the *Watunna*, I will focus on the section featuring Wanadi, the Makiritare proto-shaman, God and culture hero all rolled into one, who was created by Shi (the sun). Wanadi established order as it is known today and, since his farewell to the Earth, has not taken part in the affairs of humans. One tale in the Wanadi section, "Kaweshawa," relates Wanadi's meeting and relationship with his wife, Kaweshawa. I am using this tale for my initial study of the act of storytelling and gender dynamics in the *Watunna*.

The story centers on Wanadi and his choice of bride, Kaweshawa. Wanadi catches Kaweshawa while fishing, as she is the daughter of the master of fish. They struggle, trying to best each other, but eventually Wanadi wins and decides to marry her. He allows two friends to rid Kaweshawa of the piranhas that guard her vagina, but the two friends play a trick, as they are not castrated and therefore capable of deflowering the young virgin. Although they do deflower her, they are unable to kill the piranhas. Wanadi cures her with the juice from a vine and then takes her to her father's house. There, he volunteers to build a house as payment for Kaweshawa and promptly sets to work. Later, Kaweshawa is kidnapped by Kurunkumo, the curassow,[2] and taken to his house to be his wife. Wanadi attempts to replace Kaweshawa with four women he creates, one from white clay, one from black resin, one from a painting, and one who is a "bird woman." All four are unacceptable to him. Eventually, he locates Kaweshawa, now worn and ugly with many children. He rescues her and they flee from their pursuers. Wanadi then kills, roasts, and dumps Kaweshawa into the Lake Akuena, considered to be the lake of eternal life. She is reborn whole and beautiful. They get married and the story ends.

Using both Blanchot's theory and Silko's Native American approach to literature, we can see Wanadi as a metaphorical author and reader and Kaweshawa as a text. Wanadi, as God and proto-shaman, selects Kaweshawa as his wife. While she is a dynamic, high-spirited woman and presents several obstacles, including sexually threatening piranhas not uncommon to Native American lore, he negates these oppositions and proceeds to acquire her, at a price, from her father. In this sense, he is an intertextual author or creator pursuing a Work, the object created through interaction of author and reader of a text. He fulfills the role of creator in two ways. First, he is Wanadi, the creator of all people on the earth, including Kaweshawa. This fact is related to us in three earlier tales of the *Watunna* (See "Seruhe Ianadi," "Nadeiumadi," and "Attawanadi"). Second, he displays his authoring ability when he creates the four replacement women after Kaweshawa's kidnapping. However, these creations, or texts, are considered unacceptable, as he says, "There's no other woman for me but the first one. She's the only good one. Where is she? What am I doing looking for other women?" (de Civrieux 37).

After creating his text, Kaweshawa, he desires to become the reader of that text by possessing her, becoming her husband; however, before he is able to accomplish this task, Kaweshawa is kidnapped and taken away. (I should note that the tale explicitly states that Wanadi had not slept with her before she was kidnapped.) He must then search for her, disguise himself and enter the kidnapper's house to rescue her. The description of what he encounters explains how Kaweshawa has changed. "She was sitting there, old and dirty.... 'She's gotten really ugly,' thought Wanadi. 'She's like another woman'" (39). Wanadi is undeterred and still desires to possess her as he says to her, "'You were beautiful before. That's why I loved you. Now you're all broken down and ugly, like an old woman. You're my woman, that's why I came to get you. Okay. Let's go. I'll take you away.

Then I'll make you better'" (40). Wanadi created her, she is his text, and he does not abandon her. Instead, he rescues her, then kills and roasts her until she becomes "all wrinkled and twisted over the fire. She turned black. Her eyes were half open. She looked horrible" (42). Finally, he has her dropped into Lake Akuena, the lake of eternal life, and she comes out of the water, "beautiful and new" (43) and they marry. Through this act, he appears to successfully "read" his text, his creation, in that he is able to re-create her. For, to Blanchot, reading is the act of re-creating the text and participating as receiver of the story in Native American tradition is essential to the creation of the tale, the listener being at the least a co-author with the teller.

This depiction of Wanadi and Kaweshawa leads us to view this male-female relationship as one of man as the author and reader, and women as the text, subjected to both creation and re-creation by man. We should not, however, be so quick to finish our exploration of the tale nor ignore the mode in which it is created.

If we continue to adopt Blanchot's model of author-text-reader relationship, we must remember that the text is never passive and is the passage for the existence of the finished Work, a being created in the space between writer and reader. Indeed, when a text undergoes, or submits to, the act of reading, it is no longer an object, but undergoes a metamorphosis and possesses life. "What is a book which nobody reads? Something which is not yet written. Reading, then, is not rewriting the book, but causing the book to write itself or *to be* written—this time without the writer as intermediary, without anyone who writes it" (Blanchot, "Communication" 201). In this view, the woman as the text, through her creation and rebirth, becomes the author while the man-once-author becomes, at best, the reader or, at worst, a dismissed individual. Thus, the male paradigm of author and reader is subverted from within by the very object it seeks to create and possess in an intertextual subversion.

If we consider the possibilities of teller-listener dynamics, we have the following:

male teller, male listener
male teller, female listener
female teller, male listener

female teller, female listener

and the addition of mixed audiences for both sex tellers.

Now we can focus metatextually on the act of telling the story, remembering that both teller and listener can be either male or female. In looking at these dynamics, the intertextual subversion as Kaweshawa moves beyond her author/reader Wanadi is upheld in all four possible teller-listener sex combinations, while an additional metatextual subversion is also present that transcends the gender dynamics.

As a male or female teller creates the story anew, he or she is bringing to life, with the interaction of listeners, a tale of a male creating and re-creating a female, who then moves beyond or is moved beyond the male through the very acts of creation/re-creation. Therefore, the teller's story takes on its own life and moves beyond both author and listener to become a life of its own for one brief moment each time it is told and heard.

If a male teller relates the story, the intertextual subversion undermines his own telling, showing male creators incapable of completely capturing female creations. With a male audience, both teller and listener are mirrored in the story, providing a picture of futility. With a female audience, the male teller appears to capture himself in this futility in front of a female listener, which may show the female listener that he, at least, is aware of the limitations on male acts of creation, thus escaping in the end the inability of the protagonist Wanadi to possess his creation completely.

A female teller sharing the story must also deal with this intertextual subversion of author and listener, but perhaps can avoid the futility by using the act of storytelling to mock the male act of creation and re-creation the story relates. When relating her story to a male listener, this act could be construed as a warning not to overestimate male acts of creation or authoring. However, when sharing the story with other females, the female storyteller could create a complicit environment where all participating in the act are in agreement with regards to the limits of male creation powers.

The gender dynamics in the story and in the telling of the story appear to adopt the same fluidity as the oral tradition of the *Watunna*. Even so, we may conclude that gender relations do exist, and through a text-based analysis, we discover an indication of continual subversion of male power, disguised by authorial pursuits, by female otherness, wrapped in the covering of a text.

In any of the storytelling dynamics, we see the text still continuing on past the teller and listener to become a life of its own, much like Blanchot's Work, and also drawing in the entire tribal community for the brief instance of existence as it hangs between teller and listener. In this instance, Blanchot's Work takes one step closer to accessibility, yet is still able to remain aloof and fleeting, requiring retelling over and over again to bring it to life. This concept bolsters the Native American act of storytelling, passing the stories to generation after generation through a brief creative act repeated continually for the benefit of all in the community. In the end, we discover that the text wins out over the gender relations present and the desires of both teller and listener to capture and hold the story for longer than a moment.

Conclusion

Upon initial study, other tales in the *Watunna* lend themselves to similar discussions of gender relations and/or teller-tale-listener discussions. Much more study of the *Watunna* and the Makiritare people are needed before a clear picture of gender relations or tribal practices and beliefs regarding the act of storytelling can be created. Perhaps the use of both Native American and non-Native American literary thoughts can be used more often to critically examine such unique texts and the acts used to create them. Regardless, I rejoice in even my retelling of part of the *Watunna*, for it continues the tradition and keeps alive, through the text, the people and the Work for one brief moment.

Notes

1.   The Makiritare plant several types of yuca (alternate spelling "yucca"), a large, bush-like succulent with edible tuber roots. Two types, *manihot utilissima* (bitter) and *manihot dulcis* (sweet), provide primary food for the Makiritare. The bitter yuca planting is the cause for the celebration and retelling of the female portion of the *Watunna*. This bitter plant's roots are grated, pressed and clarified to remove as much of the poisonous prussic acid they contain as possible. Then, the resulting mash is used to make two staples of the Makiritare diet: cassava, a flat bread, and manioc, a cereal.

2 .   The curassow is a large, fowl-like game bird found only in South America.

Works Cited

Blanchot, Maurice. "Communication." *The Space of Literature*. Trans. Ann Smock. Lincoln: U of Nebraska P, 1982. 198–207.

Blanchot, Maurice. "Essential Solitude." *The Space of Literature*. Trans. Ann Smock. Lincoln: U of Nebraska P, 1982. 21–34.

de Civrieux, Marc. *Watunna: An Orinoco Creation Cycle*. Ed. and trans. David M. Guss. San Francisco: North Point Press, 1980.

Silko, Leslie Marmon. *Yellow Woman and a Beauty of the Spirit*. New York: Simon and Schuster, 1996.

4

These Were Mari Sandoz's Sioux

Malcolm A. Nelson

Mari Sandoz's *These Were the Sioux* is a short book, but a very important one to her, for, according to her biographer, she could tell things she knew about the Sioux that people would otherwise never know (Stauffer 239). That's certainly what Mari Sandoz attempted, and what I think she achieved. Yet the series the book was published in, in paperback, includes titles like *Julie Builds Her Castle* and *The Coach Nobody Liked*, obviously books for children or young adults. Other titles in the series, Mary O'Hara's *My Friend Flicka* and *Thunderhead*, young adults' books of real quality, make that even clearer. Indeed, though its aims are larger, *These Were the Sioux* does focus much of its attention on coming of age, on the education of "The Go-Along Ones," the children of the Sioux. Why should we pay attention to a book for children, however worthy or pleasing? It's a fair question, and it deserves answers.

First, children's books, at their best, may be simple but not simplistic, childlike but not childish, and worth the attention of all ages, though they may not get it: e.g., *The Once and Future King, The Hobbit, Charlotte's Web,* David Macaulay's stunning architectural books, *Alice in Wonderland.* Albert Payson Terhune's dog stories are sentimental rubbish; Jack London's are not. Coming of age stories well short of *A Portrait of the Artist as a Young Man* or *Tom Jones* can be great books.

Second, Mari Sandoz's credentials on the subject of the Sioux were formidable: vast archival research, and, more importantly, personal knowledge of the land and many of the people she wrote about. Her few playmates included Sioux children; she listened avidly to the stories of her father's Sioux friends; and, much later, she interviewed Crazy Horse's old comrade in arms, He Dog, who lived (incredibly) into the 1930s—so close are we still to that legendary time. She learned that her father's government claim on the Niobrara lay in the shadow of the hill where Conquering Bear's death scaffold had stood. Conquering Bear's murder in 1854 had begun the awful Plains wars that only ended thirty-six years later at Wounded Knee. Sandoz's father visited the site shortly after the massacre; it is less than fifty miles north of her birthplace. She says that, in her childhood, old Sioux still occasionally came to the hill "to dance a little" (*Love Song to the Plains* 179).

Child Rearing: Indian and White

Mari's friend Wallace Stegner once said that she probably would have been happier if she'd been born a Sioux (Stegner 194). Stegner's friendly joshing suggests why Mari should have found coming of age themes so appealing and treated them so knowingly and well. Her own life required her to come of age very quickly indeed—to be surrogate mother to five siblings starting when she was a scrawny child of six, after which time, as she says, she always had a baby on her hip. Mari's mother, Mary, had no time for child care. Her husband, Old Jules, used his crippled leg and his intellectual interests to avoid normal farm work—that was Mary's work, if she wanted any cash income. That left the oldest sibling—Mari—to raise the children. Any disobedience or misbehavior was quickly and brutally punished by her overbearing father. Old Jules had some admirable qualities beyond toughness, persistence, and marksmanship. Intelligence, intellectual curiosity, and respect for Indians and Indian ways were high among them. In a passage from *These Were the Sioux*, Mari, herself frightened and abused, discusses a newborn Indian baby in a lodge across the road from her house. Mari knew that the child would never receive physical punishment, for American Indians thought of European settlers as being brutal and violent toward their children (*TWTS* 20–21).

Sandoz does not understate the presence of violence and pain in Plains Indian life. The young Sioux knew physical punishment, but it came, as important lessons often do, largely from peers. She emphasizes the power of peer pressure, ridicule, and similar social sanctions in disciplining the young, "...for ridicule from the girls and women stings like the yellow-striped hornet" (*TWTS* 34). Old Jules had only contempt for his eldest daughter's literary aspirations; his preferred insect metaphor was that artists and writers were "the maggots of society" (*Old Jules* 419). Even so, Mari Sandoz did make for herself "a real place," uncommon for a woman of her time and station, stinging many targets "like the yellow-striped hornet"; not a bad metaphor for a skilled and tireless writer with an ethical agenda and a great heart.

Contraries and Deicide

Sandoz's concern that anthropologists should learn what she knew is illustrated in the following brief excerpt from her lengthy firsthand observations of the old Sioux heyoka mentioned above. The description is all the more remarkable for being so ingenuous, observations made by a little white girl with no awareness of what she was watching, no preconceptions, no assumptions, no learned reactions: "…I was stopped by the sight of an old Indian coming out of one of the tipis walking on his moccasined hands, his bare toes gesturing in the air like blunt, appealing fingers above odd noises that seemed words spoken backward…I think I laughed…" (*TWTS* 16).

A critical reader may well suspect that the mature writer has done some severe editing on the juvenile observations. Could the child really have sensed that the alien words she heard "Seemed spoken backward?" The phrase "I think I laughed" sounds very much like dim memory channeled into what the mature writer knows is the right reaction. Did the child really think of the toes as moving like fingers?

Yet her account is both powerful and precious. It proceeds at length to describe and define the nature and life of a heyoka: the puberty dream of thunder, the backwards living of life, the social value of parodies of pomposity, the simple fun of a clown's foolishness, the pathos and power of great clowning. Sandoz argues that this sort of double meaning, this ironic reversal, was typically Sioux, incorporating the ironic nature of Plains life, destruction, and creation at one and the same time. She concludes this passage with a personal recollection—how her own fear of lightning vanished in a moment when she was nearly missed while "foolishly" riding in a thunderstorm—as if this ride "had been my *heyoka* dance" (*TWTS* 18).

N. Scott Momaday is justly famous for his stunning portrayal of his Kiowa grandmother—an old woman, near death, singing prayers by her bed.

> As a child she had been to the Sun Dance…. She was about seven when the last Kiowa Sun Dance was held in 1887…. She was ten when the Kiowas came together for the last time as a living Sun Dance culture. They could find no buffalo; they had to hang an old hide from the sacred tree. Before the dance could begin, a company of soldiers rode out from Fort Sill under orders to disperse the tribe. Forbidden without cause the essential act of their faith…the Kiowas backed away forever from the medicine tree…. My Grandmother was there. Without bitterness, and for as long as she lived, she bore a vision of deicide. (*The Way to Rainy Mountain* 8–10)

Mari Sandoz gives a parallel vision of deicide in her remarkable description of a sun dance, now grudgingly permitted, but "without torture," in the early 1930s. Several people watched as the head dancer, a seventy-eight year old man, motioned to his bare breast and cried out for the thongs. But it could not be allowed. "For a moment the lean old dancer hung as from a string that did not exist. Then he crumpled down in the dust" (*TWTS* 90). People helped carry the old man to a sweat lodge, and word spread that he was alive—but his moment of hope and belief had vanished.

The sacred hoop is broken. God is dead.

Gender Roles and the Good Society

Sandoz ends her account of Sioux social patterns with a great description: "A society that has no locks can tolerate no thief; without paper…it can tolerate no liar, and no troublemaker if there is no jail…. This sense must not be that of the infant…but that of the adult, upon whose conduct all things are dependent. When men are not brave the rains fail for all, and when the women lose their virtue the buffalo do not return" (*TWTS* 43). It is easy to criticize this. It is absolute and vastly oversimplified. There must have been some thieves. The idea of "the infant" is disputable, and sounds a lot like 1940s Freudian intellectual New York City, where, in fact, Mari lived when she wrote it. Women who sleep around make the buffalo go away, right? Sure. But it's still a magnificent statement, beautiful in its absolute negative parallelisms: no locks, so no thief; no paper, so no liar; no prison, so no troublemaker. Could any society ever have been quite like that? It is good to think so.

Surely of great interest to the younger readers of *These Were the Sioux* is her treatment of "Courting the Girls." I have criticized Sandoz for her propensity to make up scenes of young boys flirting with the girls by throwing plum pits at them, then everyone blushing furiously when eye contact results. Her aim was clearly in part to counteract the whites' notion that any sexual behavior but their own (especially among the darker races) was weird, animalistic, orgiastic. She stresses the complex and restrained behavior patterns that evolved to keep peace among, say, ten or twelve people in one tipi.

It is also remarkable that she gives such a quietly sympathetic portrayal of "The woman-man, the berdache [who] was also considered of special sensitivities beyond fact and reality" (*TWTS* 56–57). Little has been written about Mari Sandoz's sexuality, and she discouraged discussion of it. She was married once, chiefly to escape her stifling home. After five years, she got a divorce, to the great shame of her mother. According to her sister, Caroline, she discouraged young women from entering into what she had found to be a confining, limiting arrangement, though she "always had a boyfriend" (Pifer). Mari argued against Freud's emphasis on the primacy of the sex drive, asserting that her upbringing had taught her that the drive for survival was a much more powerful instinct (*Letters* 38–42). There is surely no evidence that Mari Sandoz had any personal reason to sanction homosexuality, as, for example, Willa Cather would have. I have no thesis about this. I can only think how precious such frank, accepting, balanced, discussion of gender ambiguity must have been to anxious adolescents of the 1960s, and I admire Mari Sandoz for it.

It is not surprising that Mari Sandoz idealized a child-rearing system so different from the hard one that produced her. She does gloss over some aspects of Sioux culture, e.g., that vision quests seem to have been only for males. The heroes of her fine young adult Sioux novellas are male, including one who becomes tribal historian, artist, creator. Had Mari indeed been born a Sioux and a woman, she probably would not have become a distinguished writer. It would be easy to label her views of Plains Indian life rosy and uninformed.

I do nothing of the sort. Her version of Sioux life rings true both poetically and anthropologically, and the past tense of her title—*These WERE the Sioux*—is poignant in the extreme, as I am sure she intended. As she herself said in another book: "…they were a great people, these old buffalo-hunting Sioux, and some day their greatness will reach full flowering again in their children as they walk the hard new road of the white man" (*Crazy Horse* x).

Works Cited

Momaday, N. Scott. *The Way to Rainy Mountain.* Albuquerque: U of New Mexico P, 1969.

Pifer, Caroline Sandoz. Personal Interview. 15 August 1997.

Sandoz, Mari. *Crazy Horse: The Strange Man of the Oglalas.* New York: Knopf, 1942. Lincoln: U of Nebraska P, 1961.

Sandoz, Mari. *Love Song to the Plains.* New York: Harper and Row, 1961.

Sandoz, Mari. *Old Jules.* New York: Little Brown and Co., 1935.

Sandoz, Mari. *These Were the Sioux.* New York: Dell, 1961, 1967.

Stauffer, Helen Winter, ed. *Letters of Mari Sandoz.* Lincoln: U of Nebraska P, 1992.

Stauffer, Helen Winter. *Mari Sandoz: Story Catcher of the Plains.* Lincoln: U of Nebraska P, 1982.

Stegner, Wallace. *The Sound of Mountain Water.* New York: Dutton, 1980.

5

Rewriting Ethnography:
The Embedded Texts in Leslie Silko's *Ceremony*

Robert M. Nelson

It is no secret that Laguna oral traditions figure as both text and pretext in Leslie Marmon Silko's novel *Ceremony*. In interviews and elsewhere, Silko herself has often stated that the primary source of the traditional stories contained in her novel *Ceremony* is Laguna oral tradition, specifically stories she remembers hearing from her Aunt Susie and her Grandma A'mooh,[1] and most critics concede (as do I) that family tellings may well have served as source material for much of the "traditional" storytelling that shows up in the text of *Ceremony*. In fact, a few years ago another Laguna writer, Paula Gunn Allen, criticized Silko for using some of this oral traditional material, contending that by including a clan story in her novel *Ceremony,* Silko has violated local conventions regarding proper dissemination of such stories. Gunn Allen claims, I think correctly, that some clan stories simply should not be told outside the clan, let alone outside the tribe. Nor, in her view, should most literary critics deal with these pretexts in print: "I could no more do (or sanction) the kind of ceremonial investigation of *Ceremony* done by some researchers than I could slit my mother's throat. Even seeing some of it published makes my skin crawl." Moving from a critique of the critics to Silko's own writing, Gunn Allen continues,

> The parts of the novel that set other pulses atremble largely escape me. The long poem text that runs through the center has always seemed to me to contribute little to the story or its understanding. Certainly the salvation of Laguna from drought is one of its themes, but the Tayo stories which, I surmise, form their own body of literature would have been a better choice if Silko's intention was to clarify or support her text with traditional materials. [...] but the story she lays alongside the

novel is a clan story, and is not to be told outside of the clan. ("Special Problems" 382–83)

It may strike some readers as ironic that Paula Gunn Allen, who at the time of her critique of Silko had just published *Spider Woman's Granddaughters* and was about to publish the patently New Age *Grandmothers of the Light*, comes off in her argument as the defender of Laguna traditionalism and privacy against Leslie Silko's brazen affronts to them both. Irony notwithstanding, Allen raises a very serious question, one that goes to the heart of still timely issues of cultural appropriation, misappropriation, and expropriation. Were Allen correct in her contention that Silko exposes clan secrets, I for one would have equally serious qualms about undertaking to write about these pretexts.

Let me direct attention, then, to the traditional stories, or embedded texts, that do appear in Silko's novel *Ceremony*, some of which, for Allen, constitute evidence of improper publication of secret clan stories. I use the term "embedded" in part to acknowledge the way these portions of text are formally set within the matrix of the prose narrative, like bits of turquoise and coral in some kinds of Zuñi jewelry. Here I read differently from Gunn Allen, who sees these passages as lying "alongside" the novel proper, because I think they are integral to both the novel's text and texture. There are (as I count them) 28 of these embedded texts in the novel, typically typeset as though they were passages of poetry, center-justified on the page and with lines of varying lengths.

As I have already conceded, Silko may well have heard and recalled the gist of any number of such stories prior to writing the novel. But it is also demonstrably the case that at least all but two of the embedded texts in *Ceremony* are appropriated, sometimes verbatim, from preexisting ethnographic print texts rather than immediately from remembered oral performance.[2] Even if we agree, then, with Gunn Allen that the original performers and transcribers of these ethnographic works might be guilty of violations of clan secrets, the fact that such texts exist in print outside *Ceremony*, and existed well before Silko was even born, puts a very different spin on the question of cultural expropriation. Or does, at least, for me: once we concede that the pretexts for Silko's embedded texts are *printed* texts, gathered and published by both professional and armchair ethnographers before her birth, then it makes more sense to claim that in an important way Silko is not revealing or even re-revealing clan secrets but rather repatriating Laguna "artifacts," working to rescue them from their deadening status as ethnographic museum pieces and to return them to living circulation as part(s) of an ongoing, living story.

For now, though, let me propose that perhaps Silko's use of such materials is better read, not as an exploitation or improper exposure of Keresan materials, but rather as a "re-appropriation" of these previously expropriated materials, and further as re-appropriation in the service of very traditional Keresan purposes. To illustrate this proposition I will examine the function of the fragmented embedded text to which Gunn Allen refers when she writes of "the long poem text that runs through the [novel's] center [that] has always seemed to me to contribute little to the story or its understanding," the story entitled "One Time" in her 1981 book *Storyteller* (111–21). I want to show how Silko's version of this traditional Keresan story derives from ethnography but functions as a traditional Keresan storytelling trope, fulfilling the role of the "backbone" in a "body" (i.e., her novel) that preserves, by giving new life and voice to, the "long story of the People" (*Storyteller* 7).

First, let me try to "flesh out" a little what I mean, and what I think some traditional Laguna storytellers mean, when they talk about the "backbone" of a body of story. As many readers will already know, one of the recurring formal elements of storytelling in orally literate communities is the device of "framing" or "bracketing." Typically this device consists of two conventional phrases, one to mark the shift in discourse from ordinary mode to storytelling mode —as, for instance, the way the phrase "once upon a time" functions in English—and one to mark the other side of the storytelling performance, the shift from story back into normal discourse —as, for instance, the phrase "the end" functions in English.[3] "The end" still gets printed, on its own separate line and typographically center justified, at the end of many novels today; however, this and other verbal frame devices are actually superfluous in a print performance, because the two covers of the book demarcate the story "space" pretty unambiguously.[4] Such frame elements are still desirable, however, in non-print story performance, even though the exact phrases differ from community to community and even from kind of performance to kind of performance.

At Laguna, at least among the storytellers both Gunn Allen and Silko remember listening to, as well as among the informants who between 1919 and 1921 contributed the stories collected in Franz Boas's *Keresan Texts*,[5] the conventional initiator phrase of the framing pair is "hama-ha."[6] Boas's favorite translation of this phrase is "Long ago—eh!"; according to Paula Gunn Allen in *Sacred Hoop*, the phrase means something more like "long ago, so far" (147). And although neither Gunn Allen nor Silko directly mentions it, a conventional closure or terminator phrase frequently recurs as well in Boas's transcriptions of turn-of-the-century oral performance.[7] In *Keresan Texts* this phrase is given as *to·me ts'itc^c*, translated by Boas "that long it is," or (to give two typical extensions) *to·me ts'itc^{ca} s'ak'o·'ya k'ayo·tsecpi t'its^c*, literally translated, "that long is my aunt's backbone," or *to·me ts'itc^{ca} s'ak'o·'ya k'ciε·'nα k^hayo·tsecpi t^yits^c*, literally "that long is my Aunt Kachena's backbone."

The idea that there is an anatomical relationship between stories and their tellers is not just metaphor, in Keresan tradition. Silko touches on this relationship early in *Ceremony*, when a male storyteller, explaining the role of stories in preserving both the life of the People and the ceremonies, gestures to his belly and says "I keep them here / Here, put your hand on it / See, it is moving. / There is life here / for the people." Like everything else that moves and has power, a story properly understood is a living thing and is thereby related to every other living thing, sometimes overtly and directly and sometimes less obviously. A story may not always have a form that is materially palpable, like a badger or a human being does, but (like any badger or human being) any story has both a life of its own and partakes of the life it shares with all other living things: it holds a kind of life within itself, and it is itself embedded within other life. What we might call the "gist" or "essence" of any particular story, Keresan storytellers are apt to visualize as the backbone of that story, and in so doing they claim that this gist or essence is actually more substantial—denser, longer-lasting, and much less elastic—than the articulated form of this backbone, any particular verbal performance per se. It is also well to keep in mind, as this conventional Keresan closure phrase reminds an audience to do, that without a backbone there is nothing to hold a human being (or a story about being human) up straight, nothing to attach flesh to; on the other hand, given an intact backbone one can conceivably perform all sorts of cosmetic surgery on the surface version of the story that gets told, but the important thing is to work from the backbone out to the surface of things when constructing a story.

Returning now to Leslie Silko's novel and its responsibility to Keresan oral traditionalism, one might wonder that she doesn't end her written performance with a statement like "And that long is my Aunt Susie's [or my Grandma A'mooh's] backbone." A similar statement does, however, occur at the very opening of the performance, when Silko's authorial voice claims that the story we are about to enter is a project of that mother of all Laguna aunties, Ts'its'tsi'nako/ Thought Woman, and that the present storyteller is merely "telling you the story she is thinking" (1). Continuing to exercise the conventional Keresan backbone trope, working to assemble story in the way that Badger Old Man works for healing in the old stories,[8] Silko then lays out the embedded texts in her novel so that formally these "bits and pieces" of Laguna traditional story, far from being positioned peripherally with respect to the prose narrative of Tayo's adventures, rather represent the very backbone—the spinal column—of the novel, the skeleton of story that Tayo's story, the prose narrative, takes shape upon and fleshes out.

I'd like to draw attention now to the thread, or rather column, of backbone material in Silko's text that Paula Gunn Allen singles out as particularly problematic for her, that "long poem text that runs through the center [that] has always seemed to me to contribute little to the story or its understanding," and again that "story she lays alongside the novel [that] is a clan story, and is not to be told outside the clan" (383). This is the departure/recovery story that features as antagonist Pa'caya'nyi, whose introduction of Ck'o'yo medicine into the lives of the People drives our Mother Nau'ts'ity'i out of the Fifth World and down below, and as protagonist Hummingbird, who along with his sidekick Green Fly works tirelessly on behalf of the People to help effect our Mother's return. In Silko's book *Storyteller* this story, titled "One Time" in the table of contents, appears as one continuous tale; in *Ceremony*, it is cast as nine discontinuous segments, the first beginning on page 43 and the last appearing on page 256.

It is one of the more interesting examples of embedded text in the novel, both in terms of its ethnographic roots and in terms of its function with respect to the prose narrative. Like many of the embedded texts in the novel, this one is clearly a rewritten version of some classic early twentieth-century ethnography. Specifically, the text of Silko's departure/recovery tale follows closely three of Elsie Clews Parsons's transcriptions of part of the body of Laguna story published (both in Keresan and in English translation) in 1928 in Boas's *Keresan Texts*: "P'acaya´n^{y}i," "The Hummingbird," and "Origin Legend."[9]

One of the first things worth noting about Silko's redaction of these pieces of story is the way she has reassembled the record published by Boas. Boas places the episode dealing with Hummingbird's recovery of Nautsityi prior to the episode that deals with Pacayanyi's visit,[10] carefully attributing each to a different informant and attributing each with its separate title. By reversing the order of these two stories and then splicing them together, Silko at once generates a story long and complex enough to serve as a backbone for the whole novel and also recovers the departure/recovery motif that Boas's ordering disrupts.

A second thing worth noting is that although the text of Silko's performance closely follows Boas's, the texture is dramatically different. For one thing: instead of casting the text as end-wrapped prose the way Boas does, Silko "elevates" these performances to the richer-looking status of poetry, in the process adding or restoring markers of oral performance, such as line lengths consistent with phrase duration and authorial asides rendered in squared brackets. Here, as in her use of embedded texts generally, Silko is in effect working to liberate the Story of the People from the confines of Boas's rather stilted ethnographic prose. That is, she is working analogously to the way Betonie works to help free Tayo of the coyote skin in which he has been too long wrapped and trapped, or to the way Sun Man works to free the storm clouds (which are not only Sun Man's "children" but also the *shiwanna* or ancestral spirits of the People) whom Kaupata keeps locked up for several years in the northwest room of his mountain abode. Also noteworthy is the way she sequences the nine blocks of this text from one end of the body of the prose narrative to the other, like trail markers for the reader who needs periodic reassurance that the direction of Tayo's story is staying congruent with the story of Our Mother's ceremonial recovery that ontologically precedes it. Finally, of course, this retexturing of the Boas transcriptions also suggests the arrangement of the vertebrae of a backbone, embedded within and giving distinctively human form to the fleshed-out body of Tayo's prose narrative story. And in case we miss the forest here, Silko sees to it that we can see the same point in each tree: each of the fragments, center-justified on the page but composed of lines of varying lengths, takes on a suggestively skeletal appearance. Lives within lives, backbones within backbones.

But perhaps the most telling difference between Boas's and Silko's presentations of Keresan oral traditional material has to do with context. Boas presents the reader with, and I quote from his very short preface, "the following series of tales [...] collected during the years 1919–1921." Boas sorts the very miscellaneous collection of oral performances into such categories as stories, story fragments, songs, prayers, speeches, and autobiographical remarks, and he also attempts to arrange the origin and migration stories and fragments into a plausible chronological order. The gist of his closing remarks on the materials is, "well, we have all this material now, what shall we do with it?" Laguna oral tradition is presented, that is, as a quantity of collectibles. And for a collector during the 1920s, Keresan stories were becoming more valuable, because most white Americans, even the trained ethnographers among them, believed that Keresan story was dying out, that this might well be the last generation of "authentic" storytellers to gather information from.[11] Like Ishi in his glass case at Berkeley, authentic Keresan texts, like their tellers, qualified as museum pieces, and Laguna was as much an archaeological as an ethnographic site. All that's left to do now, Boas's critical apparatus in *Keresan Texts* tells us, is to pickle as many of these artifacts as we can still find in the preservative of print for future study. It is a telling comment, then, that the Boas book is out of print, impossible to come by except through special interlibrary loan. One is reminded of the boxes and boxes of human bones and "artifacts" in a museum warehouse somewhere, waiting to be sorted and displayed in the museum—or, if they get lucky, repatriated back to Indian Country.

This, it seems to me, is what Silko's presentation of these same materials amounts to: an act of repatriation, putting those Laguna bones collected by the ethnographers back to their original use—to serve as backbone for a Laguna story about Laguna life in Laguna country.

Properly speaking, in the structure of *Ceremony* the context for Laguna story is Laguna story: the "traditional" story involving Pacayanyi and Hummingbird Man traditionalizes the "now'day" story of Emo and Tayo while simultaneously the prose narrative context revives the backbone of embedded text.   In this way, the embedded texts become part of a "now'day" performance, in the process becoming as *au courant* and contemporary as the narrative skin they are in.

I want to conclude this essay by readdressing Paula Gunn Allen's comments regarding the propriety of telling clan stories to non-clan members. While I'm sure clan stories exist, I do not think that the story that appears in *Ceremony* as "the long poem text that runs through the center" is, properly speaking, just a clan story anymore. If it ever was limitedly a clan story, rather than a story common to the repertoire of accomplished storytellers of several clans, it ceased to be exclusively a clan story when, 70 years ago, a man named Ko´ᴛʸɛ, along with a man named Gʸi´mi, along with a man named Pedro Martin, shared it with Elsie Clews Parsons, who was certainly not a clan sister to any of them. Perhaps there is still a version of that story that gets told only among the members of side corn clan Kawaika; if there is, I strongly suspect no non-clan member will ever hear it told, much less ever see it in print. At any rate, the version of the story of Payacanyi and Hummingbird Man that appears in *Ceremony* is not about revealing clan secrets but rather is about re-quickening the spirit of storytelling that, until Silko wrote the novel, lay misplaced and, I would say, misrepresented in the form of the ethnographic record.

Notes

1. Susan Reyes Marmon, her paternal great-aunt; Marie Anaya Marmon, her paternal great-grandmother. On these and other family sources, see Linda Danielson, "The Storytellers in *Storyteller*" and Lee Marmon, "A Laguna Portfolio."

2. More particularly, the Keresan embedded texts derive mainly from Franz Boas's 1928 publication *Keresan Texts*, while the Navajo ones derive from Leland Wyman's translations of his and others' transcriptions of the oral component of Navajo ceremonial texts. For some discussion of the former, see Nelson, "He Said / She Said"; on the latter, see Robert Bell, "Circular Design in *Ceremony*."

3. See, for example, Helen Sekaquaptewa's opening comments on the Hopi frame elements "aliksai" and "poyuqpölö" in the videotape "Iisaw: Hopi Coyote Stories," as well as Andrew Wiget's comments on these elements in "Telling the Tale" and Larry Evers's program notes to the Sekaquaptewa video transcript. Analogously, Scott Momaday uses the traditional Towan frame elements *dypaloh* and *qtsedaba* as the first and last words of his novel *House Made of Dawn* to invoke the spirit of traditional Jemez oral performance (Nelson, *Place and Vision* 43).

4. I'm aware that attempts to subvert this convention in postwar fiction are legion. I also think most readers don't fall for it, though: what goes on before and after the first and last words of the written performance, after all, isn't copyrighted.

5. More precisely, *Keresan Texts* is Boas's edition of Elsie Clews Parsons's transcriptions of tales she collected at Laguna. As volume 8 of the Publications of the American Ethnological Society, *Keresan Texts* was published in two parts: 8.2, comprised of holographs of handwritten phonetic transcriptions of performances in Keresan of 47 stories plus miscellaneous materials (biographical tidbits about one of the informants, lyrics to several songs and chants, texts of several prayers) was published in 1925; 8.1, the English language text, was published three years later in 1928, and contains translations of the pieces in Part 2 (in roughly the same order) but also several additional fragments and a section in which Boas collates these materials with other extant ethnographic materials.

6. Boas attributes each of the stories collected in *Keresan Texts* to one of six informants, all of whom initiate at least one of their performances with the phrase "hamaha" or "hamaha-eh!" Of the 47 story texts, 36 are initiated with this phrase, while another nine include the term "hama" or "ha'ma" in their first sentence. In *Storyteller*, Silko's

Aunt Susie tells her that *"The Laguna people / always begin their stories / with 'humma-hah': / that means long ago"* (38). This phrase is still conspicuously in use at Laguna today: in 1991, for instance, a showing of 16 photographs of Laguna and Acoma old- timers mounted at the Wheelright Museum in Santa Fe by Silko's father, Lee Marmon, was titled "Humma-Ha."

7. Roughly three-fourths (35 out of 47) of the stories and story fragments given to Parsons and Boas end with some version of this phrasing, and all six informants use it at least once.

8. See, for instance, Silko's "Skeleton Fixer" (*Storyteller* 242–45) and Simon Ortiz's *A Good Journey* (42–43).

9. "P'acaya᾽ nʸi" (the orthography varies, both within Boas and between Boas and Silko) appears in both Parts 1 (13–16) and 2 (19–23), as does "The Hummingbird" (11–13, 16–18). The section titled "Origin Legend" is only in Part 1; the relevant passages are on pp. 223 ("At one time the son of the Giantess (ck`o´yo) who was called P'a´cayanʸi arrived from the north-west. He was accompanied by the Mountain-Lion-Man.... He took his flint knife and stabbed the north side of the house. Immediately water rushed out of it. Then he stabbed the west wall and a bear came out") and 226 (in which well-fed Hummingbird reveals Nautsityi's whereabouts, "in the fourth world, below," and oversees the creation of "a large fly" inside "a new jar that was covered in buckskin").

10. Here and throughout the rest of this essay, except where required by the context, I have simplified and regularized the orthography of Keresan words.

11. Perhaps this is why even living informants become archaicized in Boas's presentation: for instance, the name of one informant gets consistently spelled out phonetically as *Gʸi´mi* ("Jimmy").

Works Cited

Allen, Paula Gunn. *Grandmothers of the Light: A Medicine Woman's Sourcebook*. Boston: Beacon, 1991.

Allen, Paula Gunn. *The Sacred Hoop: Recovering the Feminine in American Indian Traditions*. Boston: Beacon, 1986.

Allen, Paula Gunn. "Special Problems in Teaching Leslie Marmon Silko's *Ceremony*." *American Indian Quarterly* 14 (Fall 1990): 379–86.

Allen, Paula Gunn. *Spider Woman's Granddaughters*. Boston: Beacon, 1989.

Bell, Robert. "Circular Design in *Ceremony*." *American Indian Quarterly* 5.1 (1979): 47–62.

Boas, Franz. *Keresan Texts*. Publications of the American Ethnological Society. Vol. 8. New York: American Ethnological Society, 1928.

Danielson, Linda. "The Storytellers in *Storyteller*." *Studies in American Indian Literatures* 1.2 (1989): 21–31.

Marmon, Lee. "A Laguna Portfolio." *Studies in American Indian Literatures* 5.1 (1993): 62–74.

Momaday, N. Scott. *House Made of Dawn*. New York: Harper, 1968.

Nelson, Robert M. "He Said / She Said: Writing Oral Tradition in John Gunn's 'Kopot Kanat' and Leslie Silko's *Storyteller*." *Studies in American Indian Literatures* 5.1 (1993): 31–50.

Nelson, Robert M. *Place and Vision: The Function of Landscape in Native American Fiction.* New York: Peter Lang, 1993.

Ortiz, Simon. *A Good Journey.* Sun Tracks 12. Tucson: U of Arizona P, 1984.

Sekaquaptewa, Helen. "Iisaw: Hopi Coyote Stories." *Words and Place: Native American Literature from the American Southwest.* Videocassette series. Prod. Larry Evers. New York: Clearwater, 1982.

Silko, Leslie Marmon. *Ceremony.* New York: Viking, 1977.

Silko, Leslie Marmon. *Storyteller.* New York: Seaver, 1981.

Wiget, Andrew. "Telling the Tale: A Performance Analysis of a Hopi Coyote Story." *Recovering the Word: Essays on Native American Literature.* Eds. Brian Swann and Arnold Krupat. Berkeley: U of California P, 1987. 297–338.

Wyman, Leland. *The Red Antway of the Navaho.* Navajo Religion Series 5. Santa Fe: Museum of Navajo Ceremonial Art, 1965.

6

Constituting and Preserving Self through Writing

Sidner J. Larson

Consistent with the authenticity debate, which seeks to define who is and who is not Indian, individuals who undertake to write about themselves have been the topic of much concern. A primary worry has to do with the reliability of the author, based on the assumption that people do not remember events exactly as they occur. According to Georges Gusdorf, for example, autobiography, "does not show us the individual seen from the outside in his visible actions but the person in his inner privacy, not as he was, not as he is, but as he believes and wishes himself to be and to have been" (45).

Gusdorf's statement assumes that events have only single, inherent meanings, rather than several meanings or perhaps no meaning at all, and that meaning is discernable only by certain people. There is the further assumption that the person has no right to see himself as he believes and wishes himself to be. These are examples of Western-style thinking that attempt to establish correspondence with absolute values, or "truths" that attempt to contain "others" as well as the constantly evolving nature of reality. For a writer of American Indian autobiography such as Barney Bush, the application of absolute principles translates very quickly into an old colonial agenda concerned with other things than truth, as when he states, "We [Indians] are exposed at the earliest ages to colonial America's truths, which are truths only as long as a group of their people have sat, debated, and philosophized long enough to satisfy themselves that this is indeed a *profitable* truth (emphasis mine)" (221).

Concern with potentially valuable territory, such as the "legitimacy" of experience, can be articulated in a number of different ways. One way is Louis Simpson's recollection: "What was I to think of the new breed of university professors, structuralists, post-structuralists, deconstructionists, who taught that experience had no meaning, that the only reality was language, one word referring to another, one 'sign' to another, with no stop in any kind of truth? Who put the word 'truth' in quotes?" (550). Simpson's remarks, generating from his experiences in war, are significant in at least two ways. First, war is probably one of the worst consequences of ideas; as well as the most dramatic illustration of the need to keep ideas grounded in actual experience—those who actually have to fight and die quickly become disenchanted with the idea of war. Second, when ideas are grounded in actual experience, certain "truths" do emerge, and they are usually less transcendental than pragmatic.

For example, Simpson points out how his wartime experience taught him affection for the so-called "common man"; taught him to value "The life of every day"; and most of all taught him his life was his own, to do with as he liked (551–52). Simpson's situation is similar to that of post-apocalypse American Indians in many ways, but particularly with regard to dealing with the aftermath of destruction. Believing one's life is one's own is important to survivors of destruction, as is believing that one's experiences have meaning. Within a situation where to live is to suffer; where to survive is to find meaning in life, Indian people often are not as interested in abstractions of experience as they are in making some sort of usable sense of their lives. Another practical example consists in how many different kinds of information can converge in ways that facilitate interpreting experience into constitution and preservation of identity. Such information often takes the forms of stories and storytelling, about which Leslie Silko has said, "you have this constant ongoing process, working on many different levels" (60). Silko privileges the pragmatic potential of storytelling, dismissing many concerns about when stories are told, or whether they are history, fact, or gossip, as not useful at the present time. On her view, what is important is the "telling," the uninterrupted flow of helpful information sent and received. Similarly, within the post-apocalypse situation of American Indians, the fact that a person would presume to tell her own stories often (not always) becomes less important than making sure they are told.

Many of the less attractive stories about American Indian experiences are usually avoided, or even suppressed. As a result, it is oftentimes left to individuals who have suffered such experiences to tell them. Robert Warrior has pointed out how, "In the concrete materiality of experience, we see both the dysfunctions colonization has created for Indian communities and the various ways Indian people have attempted to endure those dysfunctions" (183). Warrior uses a framework of intellectual sovereignty to illustrate ways to unlock the silenced voices of Indian people who still suffer with an ongoing process of genocide. Using autobiography as an example of intellectual sovereignty, Warrior interprets Jimmie Durham's assertion, "I HATE AMERICA," from his essay in the autobiographical collection *I Tell You Now*, as a courageous effort to address greed and violence associated with Indians as well as non-Indians.

In similar fashion Warrior describes Wendy Rose's essay from the same collection, "Neon Scars," as being "one of the most courageous pieces of American Indian writing of the last decade" (185). Rose takes confrontation of harsh truths a step farther, discussing in excruciating detail having been beaten and abandoned by her parents, a confrontation of domestic abuse most American Indian people would rather not talk about. Although Rose's story suggests that many Indian people are still victims of racism, violence, and the process of colonization, it also asserts the particularity of an individual's experience, deconstructing the usual general categories. Finally, and of equal importance, "Neon Scars" forces confrontation of the fact that internal oppressions are among the problems Indian people face. Facing such realities and taking responsibility for them is crucial if Indian people are to reach the next stage of their own critical process, and it is through autobiography that some of the most urgent reminders of this come clear. It was as a result of these kinds of dynamics that I wrote my own autobiography, *Catch Colt*. First, I had always found authority problematic, which I had been taught to believe was the natural consequence of being part Indian, which equaled bad seed, juvenile delinquent, half-breed, and other negative associations. I did not yet possess the words and concepts to understand that what I really resented was being defined from outside, in ways that conflicted significantly with my own internal discourse. For example, as part of the boarding school tradition of early and mid-century, I attended school off-reservation in a place that to me was much less attractive than the Fort Belknap Reservation ranch where I was raised. Furthermore, compared to my family, the individuals I met off-reservation seemed sort of pale, so to speak. Unfortunately, I often did not take care to keep my feelings to myself, and when it became clear to certain mainstream individuals that I thought more of the Indians than I did of them, they were outraged. I was constantly being told Indian people were inferior, yet from my own experience I felt very strongly they were at least equal and in many cases superior, and that created many internal and external conflicts for me.

As a result of both my bi-cultural background and my attitude, I experienced much subtle and some not-so-subtle discrimination. Some of the less apparent forms resulted in relatively simple things like getting jobs and finding a comfort level with day-to-day life being more difficult for me than they were for mainstream individuals whom I observed in similar circumstances. More blatant forms included being singled out for corporal punishment by an elementary school principal and being excluded from prestigious schoolboy activities in the town where I went to high school. Discrimination is complex, and often cloaked in the confusion of authority; furthermore, it is more often than not up to the individual suffering from inequity to deal with it on his own. The ceremony of selecting significant experiences from my life and naming them is so far the most effective means of dealing with problematic experiences of which I am aware, and serves as a useful means of unifying the past and future with the present.

Louis Simpson's recollection of academic devaluation of experience is also very familiar. The majority of my mainstream education did not address Indian experiences, a form of constructive devaluation, and perhaps it was for this reason that I found it impossible not to write my own experiences into my doctoral dissertation. Writing my own life into the dissertation met with considerable resistance, and I was counseled a number of times to discontinue the practice. I found it very difficult to do so, however, because my own experiences kept bobbing up like corks from under the mainstream material flowing over and around my life. Fortunately, I was eventually able to work out a compromise whereby I was allowed to retain some of the autobiographical material.

Not long after the dissertation was completed, I was contacted by a university press and invited to submit the manuscript for consideration. I did so, and received the almost immediate response that the press would be very interested in the manuscript if I could subordinate the academic material to the autobiographical stories. The press's reinforcement of my own intuition about the correct focus for my work was ironic, and completely opposite the university reaction, and was the first time in my life I had been officially encouraged to value my own experiences in such a meaningful way.

A positive consequence of the Vietnam war is understanding and articulation of the concept of post-traumatic stress syndrome. Understanding delayed stress reaction is a great step forward, not only for those involved in war, but for those involved in other violent and destructive experiences such as ghettoization and domestic violence. Like Wendy Rose, my mother was subjected to domestic abuse by her common-law husband. My younger brother and I observed our mother being abused when we were very young, and I am convinced that has had long-lasting effects on both of us, including a certain amount of floating anger and anxiety, some of which became directed at our mother. In addition, my biological father was not a part of my life, and I never laid eyes on him until I tracked him down in my mid-thirties. At that time I indicated I was interested in having a relationship with him and told him how to get in touch with me. I never heard from him, however, and have wondered from time to time of what elements his decisions about me consisted. On my part, some of the consequences of his decisions have to do with the necessity of undertaking certain aspects of my own parenting, which I think is paralleled by writing my own story.

It is very difficult to gauge all the consequences of such unattractive and potentially frustrating experiences, even for those who have been subjected to them firsthand. It is even more difficult for those who have not had such experiences, and as a result, many devalue, avoid, and even suppress them. Given the complex nature of negative experiences it is understandable how great the potential is for inappropriate responses, either immediately or after a delay of some time. Again, for me, far and away the most effective means of dealing with negative experiences was writing my own autobiography. In so doing, I had an opportunity to pick significant events from my life, decide whether they were negative or positive, name them as such, tally the good and the bad, and, most importantly, to feel as though I had gained control of certain events by doing these things.

The process has had some interesting results, including creating a "big picture" of my life that allowed me to see how the positive things far outweighed the negative. In addition, I found myself deciding against being too harsh toward my mother and father, choosing instead to think of them in the context of their own lives instead of as just parental figures. For example, thinking of my mother in the context of being a mixed-blood Indian woman at a time and place when it was not chic to be Indian caused me to realize immediately what a remarkable thing she had done in leaving the reservation and making a life for herself and two children.

Another thing that blossomed quickly was a sense of the tremendous resources provided by my extended family and the physical place of Fort Belknap. My family provided a generous measure of counsel, socialization, and material support throughout the years of my childhood and early adulthood. Because it was substantial and diverse, family also served as an effective buffer against all kinds of influences. During times of trouble, sorrow, illness, and defeat, as well as joy and triumph, the many levels of family enfolded, absorbed, mediated, supported, and celebrated the highs and lows associated with all our experiences.

Connection to the land is a concept that has seemed romantic and antiquated to me at times, and especially when I was trying to achieve my own independence, staying in one place seemed not useful. I begin to understand, however, the deep sense of joy and satisfaction I used to feel upon returning home after the school year. As the familiar features of Fort Belknap's Milk River valley would begin to come into view, there was a feeling quite unlike that of seeing my family again, and I now know that feeling to be a resonation to the land, light, and space of north central Montana. To be able to accept that it is possible to have a relationship with a place that is very similar to the most meaningful relationships that exist between people is to unlock a treasure chest of meaningful associations.

There is a phenomenon among Indian people that manifests itself in the ways they leave home, often for very long periods of time. American Indian intellectuals especially are known for living and working in places far removed from their places of origin, and many of these people assert that their work is helped by being conducted at a remove. At the same time, many also seem to manage to stay connected to their places of origin in extraordinary ways. Writing my own autobiography was in part an opportunity to put on paper an internal part of my life that remains very strongly connected to north central Montana. For example, I always measure where ever I am in terms of how far it is from the ranch where I grew up. I think and dream, and am reminded constantly of those early experiences, and within those senses I am still there.

External forces are undoubtedly partly responsible for cycles of movement and associated thinking, but there are also internal pressures that correspond closely to much older patterns of outward movement, such as hero stories, culminating in returning home after an arduous journey. Writing oneself is a ceremony by which the individual, incorporating internal discourse as well as outside influences, can constitute and preserve such experience; a way of tracking and articulating part of the life of the mind that also helps achieve temporal unification of the past and future with the present.

Sander Gilman recently observed, "Our awareness of how our lives and times help determine our scholarly questions has been articulated recently in a series of brilliantly written autobiographies.... These books are not simply summations of creative lives but rather rethinkings of what life events were important to the scholars and of why these events shaped the choice of scholarly field and subject" (4). This has also been the case with American Indian autobiographies that articulate how individual lives and times help determine important questions.

Autobiography provides important opportunities for grounding representation in some prior reality and for intimate expression of subjective experience, a way of making meaning out of complex reality by a combination of history and narrative. Although autobiography's self-referential connections to the world outside the text have raised questions about verifiable truth, contemporary theorists such as John Paul Eakin have turned from questions of the unreliable narrator to relations between text and reality. These relations explore issues of referentiality related to insistence on a reality external to the text, but to which the text must convincingly refer, as well as how most adequately to connect the genre of autobiography to originally lived experience. Recognizing the complex ways language structures recognition of experience, and recognizing the "self" as a linguistic and cultural construction, Eakin, in his 1992 work *Touching the World*, nonetheless resists conceiving the originating self as unreliable.

A way to begin thinking about the complexity of the interaction of life and text might be to consider autobiography an interactive genre. Interaction might be further conceived both as a way to indicate the context of life experiences and to suggest different ways to read translations of life into text. This might enable recognition of autobiographers who see their stories as more representative than personal, an example of a shift in autobiographical treatment from heroic narrative to metonymic lateral identification through relationship.[1]

This shift is illustrated in the way older autobiographies often consisted of a heroic narrative of "making it" in American culture and leaving old ways behind. Increasingly, however, "America" no longer offers one cultural ideal to seek or emulate. American national culture as well as social ideals are splintering into multiple perspectives, identities, voices, and discourses. As a result, writers are working relationally as a conjunction of cultures, working in intersections where their different backgrounds overlap. It is in these interzones where identity is being discovered and compromises or composites being negotiated. This creation is an amalgam of cultures and canons, spanned by the bridge of the self-referential, individual writer, the singular self with uniquely intercultural perspectives and experiences.

From Richard Rodriguez' *Hunger of Memory: The Education of Richard Rodriguez*, to Maxine Hong Kingston's *The Woman Warrior: Memoirs of a Girlhood among Ghosts*, to N. Scott Momaday's *The Names*, the new autobiographers have come up with various solutions to the violent wrenching from one culture to another that is so much a part of celebrating diversity. Each one, however, practices fidelity to the process of endlessly constructing and deconstructing meanings and selves, a process that is very likely one of the more important "truths" they locate.

Notes

1. Arnold Krupat, in "Native American Autobiography and the Synecdochic Self," discusses the metaphorical conception of self as well as metonymy and synecdoche as relations of part-to-part and part-to-whole. Where the self as the object of conscious and developed concern is de-emphasized, concern about the unreliable narrator is lessened as well.

Works Cited

Bush, Barney. "The Personal Statement of Barney Bush." *I Tell You Now: Autobiographical Essays by Native American Writers.* Ed. Brian Swann and Arnold Krupat. Lincoln: U of Nebraska P, 1987.

Gilman, Sander. "What Should Scholarly Publication in the Humanities Be?" *MLA Newsletter* (Fall 1995): 4.

Gusdorf, Georges. "Conditions & Limits of Autobiography." *Autobiography: Essays Theoretical & Critical.* Ed. James Olney. Princeton: Princeton U P, 1988.

Krupat, Arnold. "Native American Autobiography and the Synechdochic Self." *American Autobiography: Retrospect and Prospect.* Ed. Paul John Eakin. Madison: U of Wisconsin P, 1991. 171–94.

Silko, Leslie Marmon. "Language and Literature from a Pueblo Indian Perspective." *Literature: Opening Up the Canon.* Baltimore: Johns Hopkins U P, 1981.

Simpson, Louis. "Soldier's Heart." *Hudson Review* 49.4 (Winter 1977): 541.

Warrior, Robert Allen. *Tribal Secrets: Vine Deloria, Jr., John Joseph Mathews, and the Recovery of American Indian Intellectual Traditions.* Ann Arbor: UMI, 1993.

II

New Stories:
Modern American Indian Literatures

7

Perception in D'Arcy McNickle's
The Surrounded: A Postcolonial Reading

Jeri Zulli

Recently, postcolonial theorists have taken a new look at the way colonizing cultures have traditionally interpreted the texts produced by the colonized in a binary, us versus them, invader versus invaded, paradigm. As Anuradha Needham has articulated, these interpretations are "predicated on a more fundamental blindness that conceives of colonialism and resistance to it as monolithic, as somehow divorced from and, therefore, not affected by considerations such as gender, race, class, and other diverse material circumstances" (94). In other words, traditional critical interpretations of colonized texts either ignore that a variety of influences are at work, or presume that colonization overrides these other discourses. In "Notes on the 'Post-Colonial,'" Ella Shohat explains that postcolonial discourse "attempt[s] to transcend the (presumed) binarisms of Third Worldist militancy" (103)—where the term "Third World" represents any colonized culture. Shohat goes on to further clarify postcolonial critique "as a movement beyond a relatively binaristic, fixed and stable mapping of power relations between 'colonizer/colonized'.... Such rearticulations suggest a more nuanced discourse, which allows for movement, mobility and fluidity" (108). These new approaches provide a tool for re-examining Native American texts, texts that previously have been interpreted strictly in binary—Western versus Indian—terms.[1]

In this essay, I provide a postcolonial reading of D'Arcy McNickle's *The Surrounded*, a novel that examines the nature of the relationship between and among Native Americans and European-Americans during the early part of the twentieth century. Existing critical examinations of the novel suggest that the text considers the role played by miscommunication between the two peoples in the failure of any successful cohabitation to exist—miscommunication brought on primarily, according to colonialist thinking, by binarial differences in perception; we have the "Western" view and the "Indian" view. Existing critical analyses of the work begin with the assumption of this binarial difference in perception. For example, Dorothy Parker suggests in her biography of the author that McNickle focuses on the question: "How do people communicate (or fail to do so) across cultural barriers when language itself, the basic tool of communication, derives from radically different modes of perception?" (225). John Purdy, in his examination of *The Surrounded*, claims that, "McNickle uses the coincidence between Salish tradition and Euramerican historical record to evolve two opposing perceptions of events" (44). These readings of the text, however, limit the characters in *The Surrounded* to the binary roles of invader and invaded, further extending colonialist attitudes and reasoning and recolonizing ethnic culture through Western theory. The very title, *THE SURROUNDED*, creates a visual image that challenges suggestions of binarism. When we read from a postcolonial perspective, we can see that this text goes beyond just emphasizing the extent to which culture figures in perception. In fact, the text demonstrates the different perspectives that even people within the same culture may have of the same event or series of events. Emphasizing the importance of these differences in perception by continual use of tropes of seeing and vision, the novel debunks the myth of unity of perception that colonialist readings have forced upon this text and, hence, colonized culture.

Problematizing a "Native" Perspective

The Surrounded is the story of Archilde Leon, a half-Spanish, half-Salish man who was raised on Indian land but has lived in Western society. As the novel opens, Archilde is visiting his parents (who live on Salish lands) after more than a year away making a living in Portland. By beginning the story with an "Indian boy" (in his mother's words) returning from a Western city, the text steers the reader in the direction of a binary reading; Archilde provides a running commentary on the differences between the cultures. Throughout the text, however, Native American characters as well as European-American characters interact both within (assumed) cultural groups and across (assumed) cultural borders in ways that problematize the notion of a simple colonized/colonizer binary. Additionally, the use of the tropes of vision and seeing reinforce the breakdown of assigned stereotypical perceptions.

The Native American characters Catharine and Modeste are examples of the inclusion of diversity of perception within an assumed cultural group as a primary aspect of *The Surrounded*. Catharine, mother of Archilde, is full-blooded Salish and lives in a cabin on Indian lands in Montana. Archilde is her child by her Spanish husband, Max Leon, who, although a white man, also lives in Salish territory. Modeste—an uncle or perhaps an in-law of Archilde's—is a Salish elder also living on tribal lands. He is full of stories of older ways and simpler times.

At first glance, it appears that Catharine and Modeste share a kind of "Native vision type" of perception, leading the reader into a comfortable categorization of old Indians. Both are physiologically vision-impaired, for example: Catharine is nearly blind; Modeste entirely so. Both were raised during the time when missionaries, the "Black Robes who do not marry" came to Montana and worked among the Salish, and both have lived their entire lives on Indian lands. However, whereas Catharine embraced Christianity—albeit uncomfortably—Modeste did not. Archilde reveals that his mother feared hell above all (4). She is prone to saying things like "'Dear Jesus! Save him from hell!'" in reference to a son in trouble (20). Modeste's perception of events has never wavered from the point of view of one who tolerates Christian missionaries in his midst; as he says, "'We thought they would bring back the power we had lost—but today we have less'" (74). However, he embraces only traditional Salish values; hence, from the beginning, his perception of the "invasion" of the west has been different from Catharine's. Catharine struggles with her faith; Modeste does not. Catharine quotes Catholic dogma at her son; Modeste gives Archilde amulets, such as an eagle-bone whistle or the polished claw of a grizzly, as "safe-keepers." Catharine envisioned heavenly messiahs; Modeste's vain hope was more earth-bound. Among the elder Salish, the text, rather than providing a unity of perception, suggests a diversity in interpretation of the arrival of the colonizers.

Archilde, Catharine's youngest son, does not embrace either of these perspectives, nor is he characterized within the same parameters of tropes of seeing. In contrast to these two elders, he has "healthy" vision and is characterized almost in every scene as carefully scrutinizing whomever he is with. Eyes, seeing, vision—these play a greater role in his communication with his mother than language does, as is evidenced in a scene when he sees his mother again after an entire year apart (3). We sense that she looks no different because Archilde does not expect her to look different. This observation highlights the role of personal (non-cultural) point of view in perception, and helps reveal as a false construction the idea of a Western versus Indian polar perception; this scene introduces the role of generation and familial relationship to perspective. The scene is played out in parallel a few pages later when Archilde greets his father and hold's his gaze while trying to mask his annoyance at something his father had said (6). Again, the primary communication is not word-language but eye-perception, and it is clear that Archilde's seeing is not parallel either to his father's perception or to his mother's.

The most important scene in the novel in terms of Archilde's perception takes place when he finds Mike and Narcisse, his sister's sons, camped in the woods. Archilde realizes, "He was always forgetting that his way of seeing things was his own. His people could not understand it, but thought he was chasing after damn fool notions... . In his present evolution, he could admit this lack of insight in his people without getting angry" (247). The naiveté of this passage is important: Archilde has recognized the role played by perception and seeing in communication but has failed to recognize that his own perception is no less personal nor based solely on culture than is that of other Indians in the story, "his people." One could argue that Archilde is no longer on the Indian side of the "binary" because of so much time spent in Western schools and churches and working in the Western world, but the attraction that Archilde feels to return to his home (Indian) lands and his comfort with that environment—the fishing and camping, the homey feel of the mountains—work against attempts to define him as existing on the western "side." He is anti-binary.

Problematizing a Generational Perspective

The text does not let us settle comfortably into a generational binary, either, however, as Louis, Archilde's brother, perceives his parents and the world differently from Archilde. Louis and Archilde are both half Salish and half Spanish; but, neither can be said to represent an essentialized "half-breed" perception. According to the text, they did not seem to be brothers from their appearance, and they, too, were aware of their dissimilarity (17). In fact, the very presence of these racially mixed offspring in the novel complicates readings that would insist upon racially binary perspectives. What happens to notions of essentialized perceptions when the boundaries on which they are based start to blur? Early in his life Archilde demonstrated an affinity for music and is a fiddler for hire in "white" cities; Louis has remained on Salish lands, and, as the novel opens, is wanted for horse theft. While they appear to be set up as good brother/bad brother, the characterizations are more complicated than they appear at first glance. Although Archilde chooses to attempt to assimilate into Western culture, he recognizes the shortcomings in white relationships with Natives and bemoans them. For Louis, whites are the enemy, but his relationship with his white father is not better or worse than Archilde's—just different. The differences between the perceptions of the brothers become more important as the novel reaches its turning-point scene.

The pivotal scene of the novel, wherein the lawmen come upon Catharine, Archilde, and Louis in the woods, exemplifies the diversity of perspective, not only between Archilde and Louis, but also between and among the others in the climactic scene. Archilde has taken Catharine hunting; they are joined after a few days by Louis. Archilde warns Louis that Sheriff Quigley is searching the woods for him because of the horse theft charges, but Louis refuses to be concerned. Louis kills a deer and drags it into camp, bragging to Archilde. His brother, shamed, lies and claims to have killed a deer also, even though at the crucial moment (demonstrating a different perspective on hunting between the brothers), Archilde had been unable to pull the trigger. When the game warden shows up, Archilde does not perceive a threat. "Archilde felt at ease, though he could see that Louis and the old lady were nervous" (124).

To Catharine and Louis, "The Law [capital L] was a threatening symbol" (124). Archilde believes that by telling the truth, they can get out of the situation, fully aware that Louis is wanted for horse theft and not wanting to draw unnecessary attention. Louis is caught between fear of Western authority and unashamed youthful desire to brag about the deer that he killed and about the one he believes Archilde has killed; he does not realize that far from impressing the game warden, he is only angering him. He will not believe Archilde when Archilde admits that he did not bag a deer. Louis and Archilde perceive the situation differently, and Louis is killed for his misperception; he reaches for his gun only to tote it with him and his move is misinterpreted by the lawmen. Then, Archilde and Catharine perceive the next logical step differently. While Archilde is still trying to sort out the confusion, Catharine kills the warden before Archilde can actually see it happen. The perception of events in that scene is different for each character—and most definitely not race-specific; Archilde sees things differently from his mother and his brother; in fact, he is portrayed as understanding the warden's perception of events.

Perspectives Change

The novel also depicts changes in perception within the Salish community, further problematizing attempts to read into the text a unified Indian perspective. For example, Archilde's perception of the Salish history is not constant. At the beginning of the feast prepared by Catharine in honor of her son's return home, when the older Salish were telling the old stories, "[Archilde's] eyes saw the old faces, faces he had forgotten about, never thought to see again…" and he was impatient, bored, and unable to see beyond the physical appearances of his relatives (62). However, we see that Archilde has finally taken a step toward transcending this inability to see beyond the visible when, during a particularly compelling old tale, we are told, "For the first time, he had really seen it happen. First the great numbers and the power…. Now he saw that it had happened and it left him feeling weak" (74). Archilde's perception of events has altered.

Catharine's perception also changes. Toward the end of the novel, she begins to doubt that Christian confession is sufficient to provide absolution for her sins. Eventually her Salish faith overpowers her

Christian upbringing and she participates in a Salish ritual of self-flagellation for absolution of sin. The fact that perceptions (within a constructed cultural grouping) can evolve works against notions of perception binarism.

Problematizing the "Colonizer" Perspective

Thus far, we have examined the diversity of perspective among the Native Americans in the text. Not all who live in the Salish community, however, are Salish. In referring to the European-American characters in the novel, Purdy states that "Their vision is blind to any other perception of the world, and their place in it, for its scientific, geometrical sense of regularity is arrogantly myopic and, therefore, inflexible" (46). However, the non-Native characters in the novel do not share culture-specific perceptions. With the introduction into the story of Archilde's father, Max Leon, a Spaniard who has chosen to make his home among the Indians, the text has an additional binary-breaking character, since Max is not on either "side." He is not comfortable in any relationships with other whites, such as fellow rancher Emile Pariseau or Indian-agent-turned-merchant George Moser. Yet, neither does he feel included as part of the Indian community. Max often complains that he does not understand the Salish, even though he has lived among them for more than forty years (75). He does not understand them because he tries to put them all into a category, and they will not fit. He admits to his friend, confessor, and confidante, Father Grepilloux, that they were no different from other people, that they all had their individual characteristics, that "...there was no single trait he knew of to describe all Indians" (42). This, of course, is precisely the point. In true colonialist fashion, Max tries to categorize all the Natives, but just as his sons are different from each other, so are all Salish different from one another.

When Grepilloux dies, we as readers are privy to Max's struggle to visualize his departed friend in a moment wherein he gazes at the fresco above the altar, but it seemed out of focus and lacked meaning (135). The implication is that the Christian religion cannot supply the answers for Max, so clearly, although not "Native," Max neither embraces nor denies all the perception perspectives of either his European heritage or his adopted Indian culture. As with his wife, Catharine, the Christian religion does not provide him with all the answers. As with his son Archilde, his perspective is unique and personal. In fact, the Leon family can be seen as a microcosm of the Salish world, with its different perspectives, each member influenced not only by race but also by gender, generation, and life experiences, among other influences.

Father Grepilloux is another white character who has made his home among the Indians. Purdy suggests that Father Grepilloux's "Christian sense of order blinds his attempts to address the damage his battles have wrought" (47). However, there is a sense that the priest is aware of perception problems. While relating a story from his memoirs, the priest suggests that he realizes that no human possesses the absolute perception path to truth. The memoirs he shares with Max offer an alternate view of historical events to those described at the feast, and to any authoritative (colonizer-provided) text, even in terms of his choice of topics. The difference in perspectives between these two westerners—the priest and Max—and, complementarily, their difference in perspective from the lawmen, emphasizes how naive it is to suggest that this is a story of binary perspectives. The "lawmen"—the game warden, the agent Horace Parker, the Sheriff Dave Quigley—do seem to share an occupation-specific perspective, but not necessarily a race- or culture-specific one.

There are others in the novel who are not Native Americans and are depicted with diverse levels of seeing and not seeing; their characterizations also belie binary readings of us versus them perspectives. For example, George Moser, local merchant, tries hard to befriend "fellow white man" Max Leon, but fails miserably. Moser is relatively content living among the Salish, but his wife is not. She most decidedly sees them as "other," and nags him about going home; her characterization provides evidence of diversity of opinion within her (white) cultural grouping. In examining the non-Indian characters, it becomes increasingly clear that attempts to suggest a unified "Western" or "white" perspective only extend the misreading of colonizer versus colonized to do an equal injustice to the "majority" or "First World" culture.

Conclusion

In order to understand more fully the dynamics at work both within the colonized culture and within that of the colonizers—as well as cross-culturally—we as readers need to avoid binary polarization and move toward less essentialized interpretations of Native American texts. If we continue to read these texts as indicative of binary perspectives, we relegate the colonized culture to something only perceivable through the lens of colonization, only understandable through the eyes of majority culture. Clearly, *The Surrounded* complicates our understanding of racial perception essentialization and dispels notions that the colonized and the colonizers constitute binary, opposed perceptions.

Notes

1. For further discussion of this binary and the interrogation thereof, I refer the reader to Frederic Jameson's "Third World Literature in the Era of Multinational Capitalism" and a response piece that appears as a chapter in Aijaz Ahmad's book *In Theory*.

Works Cited

Ahmad, Aijaz. *In Theory*. Oxford: Oxford UP, 1992.

Jameson, Frederic. "Third-World Literature in the Era of Multinational Capitalism." *Social Text* 15 (Fall 1986): 65–88.

McNickle, D'Arcy. *The Surrounded*. 1936. Albuquerque: New Mexico U P, 1978.

Needham, Anuradha Dingwaney. "At the Receiving End: Reading 'Third' World Texts in a 'First' World Context." *Women's Studies Quarterly* 18.3–4 (Fall/Winter 1990): 91–99.

Parker, Dorothy R. *Singing an Indian Song: A Biography of D'Arcy McNickle*. Lincoln: U of Nebraska P, 1992.

Purdy, John Lloyd. *Word Ways: The Novels of D'Arcy McNickle* Tucson: Arizona U P, 1990.

Shohat, Ella. "Notes on the 'Post-Colonial.'" *Social Text* 31–32 (Summer 1992): 99–113.

8

Teaching Leslie Marmon Silko's *Ceremony*

Conrad Shumaker

Ceremony is one of those rare books that change the way people think about the world. In the reading journals they keep for my classes, students often report that Silko's novel has given them a new way of seeing their own culture, allowed them to understand nature differently, or provided a language in which to express intuitions they had no words for previously. An honors student even told me that he had to stop reading one night because he realized with a sense of shock that he would not be the same person when he finished the book.

I think the work has this effect in part because of what it tells us about our own culture. Though it focuses on a Laguna man's rediscovery of his people's traditional values, *Ceremony* also provides a way of seeing European-American values in a new light. It offers an alternate view of the world in prose that is strikingly beautiful and deeply resonant, and that vision, emerging as it does from a tradition that emphasizes the connections between all things, highlights by contrast the isolation and separation our students often feel as "Americans."

At the same time, the book's very strengths present real challenges to anyone who would teach it. Like it or not, the modern university and to some extent our approach to teaching literature have emerged from the view of the world the book criticizes. The problem was stated quite succinctly by a bright student the first time I taught *Ceremony*: "Why," she asked, "are we *analyzing* this book?" She had seen immediately the contradiction between the novel's emphasis on connected wholeness and an approach to literary study which seems to focus on "untying" the whole and studying the parts. In this essay I want to explore some of the implications of that student's question. I begin by discussing briefly the view of the world Silko develops in the novel and the particular challenges that view presents. Then I'll suggest an approach to teaching the work that has evolved (and is still evolving) out of several years of experience. Along the way, I hope to show how thinking about teaching *Ceremony* might help to clarify just what we try to do when we teach literature in general.

This "Fragile" World

Silko introduces her complex view of the world most clearly near the beginning of the novel, when old Ku'oosh, a Laguna holy man, tries to help Tayo, the mixed-blood hero of the book who is recovering from his experiences in the United States Army during World War II. As he tries to show Tayo how he could have been harmed by participating in the war, Ku'oosh uses complex sentences with their own meanings to suggest that whatever he said was only a sequence of repetitions. Then he pauses. "But you know, grandson," he says, "this world is fragile." The passage that follows this remark is central to the novel. The narrator tells us that, paradoxically, the word he uses to express "fragile" is "filled with the intricacies of a continuing process, and with a strength inherent in spider webs woven across paths through sand hills where early in the morning the sun becomes entangled in each filament of web." Ku'oosh tells Tayo that this fragility and intricacy are hard to describe in words, because "no word exists alone, and the reason for choosing each word had to be explained with a story about why it must be said this certain way." In spite of the difficulty, the explanations must be made, because, according to Ku'oosh, each word has its own story, and each story must be told so that there is no mistaking each word's meaning. "[A]nd this demanded great patience and love" (34–35).

The imagery of the spider web and the emphasis on stories here remind us of the book's beginning, where we are told that "Thought-Woman, the spider," created the world by thinking and that she is thinking now of the story that the narrator will tell us. Throughout the novel, in fact, we are shown that the world is made of and by stories, which, like the spider web, catch the light in their resilient strands but can be broken. And like the strands of the web, each word or sentence has meaning only in relationship to other words and stories, and only insofar as a teller ensures that the listener understands the relationship between words and meanings, stories and the world. Teller and listener are thus connected by the love inherent in the process of understanding. And like the spider's web, each story embodies a pattern that is independent of any individual weaving, but exists uniquely in the relationship created by each telling. Finally, the webs are woven across paths, strands of a larger web, the pattern of past, present, and future journeys, the people walking on the earth. The webs on the path thus connect all the elements of the Pueblo world—the hills, the sun, the movement of people on the land. Furthermore, through the story of Thought-Woman, which we bring to the image of the webs, we are connected to the history of a culture with its stories of the world's creation. It is this sense of connections, of a fragility that is also a strength, that informs Silko's novel and her view of the world. To be human is to recognize and take responsibility for this peculiar fragile strength of the world and of the stories that make it.

The contrast between this view and the Euroamerican model of the world provides the foundation for much of the novel's action. As Helen Jaskoski has pointed out, *Ceremony* highlights two very different ways of understanding the world: "Native American thought…seeks understanding that is holistic and integrating…. The Western—European or Euroamerican—world view, by contrast, tends toward atomism and the disintegration of dissection and calculation" (5). White doctors have tried to cure Tayo of what they call battle fatigue by separating the tangled threads that bind his experiences to those of others. They give him "facts" about the separation imposed by time and space: His uncle Josiah could not have been on a Pacific island when American soldiers executed Japanese prisoners; Tayo's cursing of the rain in the jungle could not cause a drought thousands of miles away. They tell him that he has to concentrate only on himself, because thinking of the others and not himself would prevent his healing (Silko 125). For the doctors, the connections he sees are neurotic or pathological, and he must conceive of himself as an individual whose problems are not those of the land or of other people. Tayo tries to believe them, but at some level he knows that "the world didn't work that way. His sickness was only part of something larger, and his cure would be found only in something great and inclusive of everything" (126).

This opposition between the white and Indian views of things is repeated at every level. Again and again we see that Euroamerican culture works to separate things, to deny that the world is the fragile web of connections that Ku'oosh describes. Mainstream American culture has its one story, in which the individual "succeeds" by denying precisely the connections that give meaning to the Indian world. Tayo's mother and then his cousin Rocky drift away from their people and finally die because they try to live that story. Christianity, we are told, separates the individual from the clan (68). Perhaps the most disturbing version of this message is the one embodied in education. At schools run by "holy missionary white people who wanted only good for the Indians," promising children are told, "don't let the people at home hold you back" (51), and white science teachers dismiss as "superstitions" the stories that connect the Indian children to nature. When the Navajo students are horrified by the sight of the dead frogs they are supposed to dissect in biology class, for example, the teacher laughs so hard that "he even had to wipe tears from his eyes" (195). For the Navajo children the frogs are related beings whose mistreatment will have consequences; for the white teachers they are disconnected objects of study, and dissection is a necessary rite of passage into a universe of objects. Moreover, when they attack the stories that protect frogs, the teachers destroy the children's connection not only to the natural world but to their parents and their culture. In a perfect illustration of Silko's view, the scalpel that severs the sinews of the frog also cuts apart a whole people and the stories that make their world.

The ability to separate things apparently gives the whites great power. Because we don't acknowledge the same kind of connection to the land, the plants, the animals, or other groups of humans, we can use them seemingly without limits, creating wealth and luxuries that tribal cultures never dreamed of. But we also become destroyers who know and use only fragments, cutting them away from the whole and often causing the death of what we touch.

Indeed, according to the Navajo shaman Betonie, Europeans were invented by Indian witches as tools who would provide the dead bodies that witchery thrives on. Having grown away from the earth, the sun, the plants and animals, they see a world of objects that are not alive. The four lines of Betonie's story that sum up the characteristics of white culture are chilling in their implications:

> They fear
> They fear the world.
> They destroy what they fear
> They fear themselves. (135)

In this view of things, white people are not inherently evil. The destructive aspect of our culture is simply a powerful embodiment of the urge within all humans to gain power over the world by treating it as separate and fragmented. Whites, Silko insists, become the primary victims of that power, suffering from "the dissolution of their consciousness into dead objects: the plastic and neon, the concrete and steel" (204). "The only cure," we're told at the beginning of the novel, "is a good ceremony"—a recognition and acting out of the connections that shape our lives. As Louis Owens has shown, it is by learning to love Ts'eh—a living woman who is at the same time Yellow Woman from traditional stories and the embodiment of the land itself—and by seeing how the stories interweave and become the story that is still being told today (Silko 246), Tayo is healed and "will succeed in restoring balance to his world" (Owens 187).

The World of the University Classroom

However, picture the world of separation and specialization into which the teacher brings this novel. The classrooms in which I teach are gray rectangles of concrete block, their space separated as carefully as possible from anything that might distract the students' attention. Their shape and arrangement proclaim the separation between the specialist and the students he or she lectures to—students sit in lines facing the front, and in order to see each other they must struggle against the very design of the room. And this classroom lies within a battleground on which relationship has long been losing to specialization. In the last five years at the university where I teach, the College of Sciences and Humanities has been divided into three colleges, all competing with each other for resources. Despite praiseworthy efforts by organizations such as the American Culture Association, most universities seem to give lip service to "interdisciplinary studies" while the disciplines in the university are actually moving away from each other like the galaxies in the universe.

Of course, people like me are contributing our share to the isolation. Movements in literary criticism that started out attempting to place the text in the world from which the excesses of "New Criticism" threatened to remove it have become so highly specialized that many of us write for tiny audiences in language that baffles and repels the uninitiated. Pressure to publish creates "original" readings of works—often highly individual interpretations having little to do with the shared experience of stories. And the system doesn't give us time for the kind of understanding old Ku'oosh speaks of—we have to cover the period so our students will succeed on the Rising Junior Exam or the GRE.

The result of all this is that students have often been taught to approach literary works as puzzles existing in a void. I have found that many of them don't expect to understand the literal level—the story—in the works they read. Since everything means something else in a work for reasons they don't quite understand, the important thing is to "interpret," i.e., discover a mysterious meaning for each part of the text without worrying too much about the story. You may have seen the humorous discussion of how to succeed at college that has been circulating on e-mail, in which students are advised to approach texts in their English classes by affirming that nothing is what it seems to be. "Don't say that Moby Dick is a whale," the author advises, "say he's the Republic of Ireland." This line, I fear, exaggerates but captures all too well a common student perception about the mysterious way their teachers derive "meaning" from a literary work. Literary analysis seems to mean finding a meaning for each part so we don't mistake the work for a story.

Rebuilding the Web

I can't claim to have found a solution to all these problems, but thinking about them has, I believe, led me to some discoveries. The first is that "analysis" is an inappropriate term for what most of us are trying to do as teachers and scholars. The more I reflected on my student's question, the more clearly I realized that true literary study consists not of breaking apart but of making connections. When we ask, "Why this word?" what we mean is "How does this mean in relation to the story, to everything else in the work? What other stories does this image bring to the work, and how can we tell those so that others will see the connections?" No word or image or story can be known by itself. We are not laboratory scientists dissecting dead bodies in order to determine the function of parts. I think that on our best days we are more like Ku'oosh as he tells the stories about "why things must be said this certain way."

So the major problem, I think, is to make this clear to students. I most often discuss *Ceremony* in a sophomore honors course on "The Cultures of America," which I team teach with Patricia Washington McGraw, an African-American professor who fortunately is quite an imaginative teacher and willing to try new approaches. After we spend about two periods introducing the novel and helping students deal with the difficult narrative voice of its opening sections, she and I divide them into groups of four or five and tell each to begin at a designated *place* in the novel—a particularly meaningful or significant scene or episode. Their instructions are first—and primarily—to explore the place and discover how it is connected to its surroundings—other major scenes in the book. What is its place in the story? If their scene seems particularly closely tied to that of another group, we encourage them to talk to that group. Then they are asked to make connections between *Ceremony* and Native American stories we have read earlier—a selection of creation, trickster, and hero stories from various cultures. We also ask them to think about connections to other works we have read: African and African-American myths and tales, works by such Euroamerican icons as William Bradford, Hector St. Jean de Crevecoeur, and Benjamin Franklin, and Ralph Ellison's *Invisible Man*. Once they have finished reading the novel, they are assigned short works by Gary Soto, Amy Tan, Jimmy Santiago Baca, Michael Anthony, and others, and they are asked to see how those works connect with *Ceremony*. Finally, we ask them to think about how the novel might have shed light on other courses they are taking and on their own experiences. We tell them that they can present their results to the class in any way they choose, and we encourage them to be creative, to think of presentation strategies that fit what they have discovered about their reading. Then we let them talk: We simply wander around the room to answer questions and ensure that the groups stay focused. They do. In fact, most of them take their discussions outside the classroom and spend quite a bit of time on their own planning their presentations.

Interestingly, many of those presentations become ceremonies involving—sometimes literally—the creation of webs, the acting out of relationships among people and literary works.   Students discover connections between the Cherokee story of the Bear Man and the scene in which Tayo and Rocky kill the deer. They discover witchery in Ellison's *Invisible Man.* If they are from rural areas or small towns, they find that they too have been told "Don't let the people at home hold you back." This doesn't mean, of course, that they are allowed to ignore differences between cultures. We help them see that the vision of *Ceremony* arises from a particular culture and that we must remember that our assumptions may differ from those of the writers and characters we study. Nevertheless, *Ceremony* becomes the center of threads that pull together the works they have read in the course of the semester.

All this takes time: We devote at least three weeks to our discussion of *Ceremony* and are prepared to spend even more time if necessary. As Ku'oosh says, understanding the stories takes great patience and love. Once students start discovering connections, it can be hard for them to decide how to limit their presentations. Among other things, they learn that any approach to a work of literature must limit and select in ways that don't distort the whole. But by the end of the presentations I think the class is much more closely knit and has a sense of how the whole course fits together, how all the stories are part of the same story and how that story is the one they are living. If nothing else, I hope, *Ceremony* enables them to see that stories are central to our identity and that understanding them doesn't mean taking them apart or finding an interpretation that no one else could possibly arrive at.   Ideally, they learn to hear the echoes and resonances among the stories and to find themselves within them.

Works Cited

Jaskoski, Helen.   "Thinking Woman's Children and the Bomb."
    Explorations in Ethnic Studies 13 (July 1990): 1–24.

Owens, Louis. *Other Destinies: Understanding the American Indian Novel.*
    Norman: U of Oklahoma P, 1992.

Silko, Leslie Marmon. *Ceremony.* New York: Viking, 1977.

9

Western Fictions in Welch's *Fools Crow*:
Languages of Landscape and Culture

Blanca Chester

> *There is so much more than just the story*
> *and what was said that is the story.*
> *Greg Sarris*

James Welch's novel, *Fools Crow*, both resists and restructures the making of history and of genre in its construction of a fictionalized account of nineteenth-century Blackfeet life. The novel ends with the slaughter of 173 Blackfeet men, women, and children on the Marias River in 1870.[1] Historical facts thus bleed into fiction. It recuperates a worldview of American Indians—more specifically, the Blackfeet—in a way that makes whites feel like outsiders to their own (constructed) history. Welch takes the history of high school textbooks and popular American myth and turns commonly accepted versions of historical events upside down. He humanizes the Indian victims of a bloody history and reveals a vital Native culture through Indian characters that contrast with stereotypical representations of the "Indian" lying in the white imagination. Finally, Welch defamiliarizes the language, culture, and historical events that characterize non-Native perceptions of Blackfeet life. He recontextualizes these through the point of view of the Blackfeet themselves and creates a dialogue between two historically clashing cultures.

Fools Crow opens by suggesting connections and differences between "us" and "them" in terms of the conventions of "the Western" and "the Indian" novel. The narrator describes a chilly autumn dusk where it is "almost night." The evening is marked by the presence of the moon, "furious" black clouds, and warm cooking fires. However, where one would expect a group of cowboys sitting around a campfire, the language signals something other than this expected convention of the American West. The name of White Man's Dog signals that this is a Western populated with Indians. Indeed, cowboys are lacking in *Fools Crow*. The Indian point of view prevails, and whites (including white readers) become outsiders; they are required to play Indian as they enter into the world of the text. Furthermore, white readers also read *Fools Crow* as outsiders to a novel that is constructed differently from conventional Westerns in other ways. As Jane Tompkins notes, most Western novels and films signal the ominous presence of Indians with their general absence. Moreover, when the Indians do turn up in Westerns, they often become part of an externalized landscape rather than fully developed characters. Here the landscape functions as a character, and both landscape and Indians make up the foreground of experience.

Fools Crow sets both the time of history and the space of the novel into a distinctly Blackfeet, or Pikuni, context. It recovers or re-coups a wealth of cultural information which is embedded so deeply in the writing that the white reader is required to do some homework in order to comprehend the larger story. In fact, unless the reader of *Fools Crow* is Blackfeet him- or herself, it is likely that much cultural information will be missed or glossed over. In the process of trying to glean a sense of understanding from out of the text, therefore, non-Native readers must construct meaning(s) from out of a kind of cultural unintelligibility.

A large part of *Fools Crow*'s unintelligibility resides in the landscape and the language of the book. This is a landscape that, in the latter half of the twentieth century, the setting of Welch's first novel, *Winter in the Blood*, Louis Owens describes as "bleak"—a "Montana wasteland." Owens describes this landscape as "dislocated" as its Native peoples (128). But in *Fools Crow* Welch transforms this apparently desolate land into the "Backbone of the World." The "bleak" Montana landscape of the twentieth century is embedded in a vital nineteenth-century culture of a people and the stories that they tell. It is alive. Moreover, dreams and stories work with the landscape to touch the lives of people directly.

Dreams are intimately connected with the land and the well-being of those living in it. The elder Yellow Kidney is disturbed by the implications of Fast Horse's dream about finding and dislodging a particular rock which covers a stream; the dream is a "complication" to the success of their mission, stealing Crow horses, and Yellow Kidney works hard to overcome his sense of foreboding. The dream later becomes a foreshadowing of more general disaster and tragedy, to be played out at the end of the novel. Yellow Kidney asks himself: What if they cannot remove the rock Fast Horse dreams about? What if they cannot find the precise ice spring along the side of Woman Don't Walk Butte? (14). Yellow Kidney's concerns suggest the inseparability of people and place, of the power of dreams and stories to construct realities for both land and people. They also suggest a time and place where, as Lee Irwin states, "There is no distinct separation between the world as dreamed and the world as lived" (18). The separateness of dreams and reality is taken for granted by most non-Natives of North America. For them dreams are symbols of an unintelligible or unconscious reality, a reality where a dream's meaning remains disguised and unintelligible to the conscious mind.

As Reed Way Dasenbrock argues, however, the fact that something is not immediately transparent or intelligible does not mean that this thing is meaningless. Dasenbrock makes this point in relationship to reading what he calls "multicultural" texts written in English, but his argument may be extended to other kinds of cultural unintelligibility. If I do not understand the importance of Fools Crow's dreams and visions, or the traditional stories that the novel incorporates into the narrative structure, this does not render them meaningless. In fact, what is least understood about them may be integral to the novel's meaning(s). According to Dasenbrock, part of what makes a "multicultural" text meaningful is its unintelligibility. The separation of "understanding" from "meaning" shows how meaning may be inherent in certain sorts of *not* understanding, particularly when a reader's relationship with a text is crosscultural. Unintelligibility leads to the reader's struggle with culturally different points of view, language differences, and other perceived gaps—the difference of the landscape, for example—in the writing. The reader has to work hard to create meaning from the text.

Metaphoric translations of the Pikuni language mark a cultural and linguistic gulf that Welch self-consciously constructs as a type of meaningful unintelligibility. "Almost night"; the "Backbone of the World"; "the Star-that-stands-still"—these sorts of phrases signal a shift in world view. This is an American Indian text written in English. At the same time, this linguistic strategy prevents the exoticization or dichotomization of American Indian experience. If numerous phrases and words were rendered in Blackfeet, rather than translated, in the way that "Napikwan," the word for white men is used, the Blackfeet point of view could more easily be dismissed or relegated to the experience of "other." Instead, "Napikwan," stands out so that *white* perceptions are consistently othered. Welch in this way insists on non-Native participation in Blackfeet history, a twist on the incorporation of the Native, as secondary, into mainstream (white) American history. The unintelligibility that *Fools Crow* confronts the reader with points to the limits of translating between cultural knowledges. However, it also points to the importance of struggling with the boundaries of such knowledge and creating new cross-cultural dialogues.

By translating a familiar English language into something unfamiliar— "hoots-in-the-nights" instead of owls—Welch makes the reader examine his or her own presuppositions about the world, and the language that links the world to some sort of reality. The English translations draw in the white reader who, ironically, remains unable to translate Blackfeet experience into anything he or she is familiar with. Paradoxically, the English language alienates the English speaker/reader. Moreover, the translations suggest Welch's own mixed background: complete translation is possible only if one is fully part of two worlds of experience, linguistically *and* culturally, and this, of course, is finally never possible. As Louis Owens notes, Welch's use of language makes English "bear the burden of an 'Other' experience" (157). The consistently othered quality to Welch's language functions through his use of metaphor. Using metaphor cross-culturally shifts the semantic fields that create paradigms of cultural knowledge. Western (European) knowledge of Native American Indian culture and history is not objective "fact." *Fools Crow*'s play with the English language shows how knowledge is constructed linguistically, how it is never neutral, and from whose point of view it has been constructed in the case of the Blackfeet people.

The impossibility of comfortable cultural and linguistic translations—one-to-one correspondences between languages and cultures—suggested by Welch's metaphorical language also emphasizes the impossibility of setting up neat dichotomies between "us" and "them," "white" and "Indian." It suggests a slippage between cultural meanings, where one term slides into the other, and where dusk can never be quite the same as "almost night." As a way of negotiating this slippage between worldviews, one focuses on the slippage itself, and on how that slippage constructs its own semantic fields. Narrative and story cannot bridge the gap between the Backbone of the World and the Black Hills of the Western frontier imagination, but they do provide a way of connecting and thinking about two distinct ways of viewing the world. Clearly, a large part of the cross-cultural experience of *Fools Crow* is the novel's insistence on the power of the word. Welch draws on the power of the oral tradition to use storytelling to re-create different worlds of experience. The power of this tradition is perhaps best summed up by N. Scott Momaday, who says, "My words exist at the level of my voice. If I do not speak with care, my words are wasted. If I do not listen with care, words are lost. If I do not remember carefully, the very purpose of words is frustrated" (160). Part of the power of oral storytelling lies in the storyteller's interactions with his audience. Written versions of stories tend to freeze narrative, preserving one version as a singular form. They tend to extend to one specific version the label "authentic" or "original." They thus suggest stasis, or product over process. In contrast, oral stories are constantly changing and evolving, like language and life itself.

The power of storied repetitions lies in their ability to invoke both story and the specific history of the telling of that story. These are stories telling stories about themselves. In fact, novels written by American Indian authors do the same thing: they tell stories about the cultural shift from oral to written forms. These writers tell stories about telling stories; they embed history in the telling of the stories themselves. These stories, like their oral counterparts, will never be finished. Their telling, like the stories from oral tradition, has no ending, a point that is also made by Welch's narrator (7). Incomplete stories suggest incomplete histories. It is in their telling that the gaps pick up meaning and become, paradoxically, complete at the same time. *Fools Crow* is simultaneously a complete and incomplete story. Its structure is novelistic, with a beginning, middle, and end. But it is also a story where the history of its characters, its people, is unfinished.

Fools Crow's vision suggests the possibility that, in the future, the blackhorns would come back (391). While this utopian dream of the past may not be a literal possibility, and Welch's use of the past tense seems to undermine its sense of optimism, this ending may still be read as recuperative. In the oral tradition it would not be an ending at all. The story of the Blackfeet continues. One is reminded of Okanagan storyteller Harry Robinson's insistence on "getting the story right" when narrating stories for the books *Write It on Your Heart* and *Nature Power*.[2] Getting the story of *Fools Crow* right means getting history right, getting the names of people and places right, and getting the words themselves right. Getting the story right is, paradoxically, never a completed act. Getting it right means telling the story again and again, in a never-ending cycle of recursivity.

Names, places, and stories act as mnemonic devices. They function as rem(a)inders of history. The traditional stories embedded in *Fools Crow* are also recorded in sources like George Bird Grinnell's *Blackfeet Lodge Tales*; Grinnell, a white man, recorded his stories about characters such as Mikapi, Red Old Man and Star Woman, and the life of the Blackfeet Indians, early in the twentieth century. These traditional Blackfeet stories remain, as Welch's narrative suggests, embedded in the oral history of the Blackfeet; they are not anthropological artifacts. Ironically, Welch re-writes stories recorded by a white anthropologist and re-inserts them into a new Blackfeet context—an American Indian (Blackfeet) novel. The stories' migration [3] resembles the sort of movement and circulation common to them in oral tradition. In this instance they have "migrated" to a novel and shown up as new written forms.

The story of the two brothers in *Fools Crow*, for example, resembles stories told in many parts of North America, including Northern British Columbia (Dunne-za),[4] and southern British Columbia and northern Washington, as told by Okanagan storyteller, Harry Robinson, in *Write It on Your Heart*. In this story one brother deceives the other and deserts him, ostensibly leaving him to die on an uninhabited island (*Fools Crow* 195–99). Through a series of deceptions, events do not turn out as planned, and the "good" brother lives while the "bad" brother is the one who becomes exiled and dies. In Welch's version, Akaiyan, the good brother, becomes the keeper of the Beaver Medicine bundle. This bundle has been handed down through Boss Ribs' family since that time; it is Boss Ribs who tells the story to Fools Crow. The link between the traditional story and the lives of people and the events that take place in the Blackfeet world is direct. The traditional stories resemble Blackfeet perceptions of the landscape; they reformulate themselves to fit into their context because they are inseparable from the people of whose lives they are a part. The stories constantly circulate and change, even in the context of a highly literate tradition.

As Arnold Davidson argues in *Coyote Country*, the linking of history and story in Native literature often transforms itself into an epic of loss. Davidson suggests this in relationship to novels such as Rudy Wiebe's *The Temptations of Big Bear* and *The Scorched Wood People* (22). These novels focus on what the Indians lost after the Europeans arrived. They contrast with those (white) epics of victory that represent how the West was "won." *Fools Crow* resembles Wiebe's epic novels in its structure; it too may be read as an epic of loss. However, the recuperation of history that Welch attempts in his re-visioning of the life and times of the Blackfeet, leading up to and including the (real) historical events of the Marias River Massacre, also suggests, as Davidson argues, a move from (patriarchal) monologue towards narrative. Narrative, or narration, as an alternative to monologue, implies dialogue. As *Fools Crow* moves from monologue to dialogue, however, it does so not only in the Bakhtinian sense of dialogism. *Fools Crow* shifts not only between individual voices, but between larger written and oral traditions. Stories, visions, and dreams suggest a cross-cultural dialogue where the oral seeps into the written text and the written text recontextualizes oral tradition. Moreover, the two exist on a continuum. Conventions from both oral and written discourse are embedded in the novel—the storytelling context of the Blackfeet and the written genre conventions of the historical and Western novel. The shifts between oral and written reveal slippages between cultures, languages, and genres of expression.

As Welch re-presents history from the perspective of the Blackfeet, the reader reconstructs and visualizes a time and a way of life that no longer exist. The initial image of the Indian that *Fools Crow* constructs resembles Daniel Francis's distinction between the Native or aboriginal person and the European construct Francis describes as the "imaginary Indian" (9). This Indian "began as a white man's mistake, and became a white man's fantasy" (Francis 5). Indians then became "anything non-Natives wanted them to be" (Francis 5). The fantasy usually played itself out as a dichotomy: the Indian as noble savage or as bloodthirsty savage. As the reader moves back in time in novels like *Fools Crow*, however, the sense of these two imaginary alternatives becomes less and less hegemonic. The reader is, instead, both drawn into another worldview and simultaneously cannot lose sight of the differences between dominant American culture and the culture of the Blackfeet. The reader is drawn in but not absorbed into American Indian identity.

While Francis notes that, "A modern Indian is a contradiction in terms.... Any Indian was by definition a traditional Indian, a relic of the past.... The image could not be modernized" (59), Welch constructs an image of the pre-modern Indian which, while "traditional" in the Blackfeet sense, does not resemble the stereotypical white image of the traditional Indian. None of Welch's characters is simple enough to slot into the categories of either/or—noble savage or barbarian. Instead, the tension between various *individual* Indians becomes apparent early in the novel when the narrator relates the elder Yellow Kidney's unease with some members of his raiding group, and his tacit approval of others. He thinks to himself, "These are good human beings...not like Owl Child and his bunch.... He had been hearing around the camps of the Pikunis that Owl Child and his gang had been causing trouble with Napikwans. It would only be a matter of time before the Napikwans" (16).

Neither Indians in general nor the Blackfeet as a group are homogenous. The alienation of Owl Child and his small group from the larger context of Pikuni tradition, however, presents a threat to the overall survival of the Blackfeet, as Yellow Kidney observes. Owl Child's hatred of the white man is a feeling shared by many of the Blackfeet, but this hatred, in Owl Child's case, is not an index of his allegiance to his own community. His alienation is complete: Owl Child exists on the periphery of two worlds, his destructive force touching white and Pikuni alike. Fools Crow thinks of him as, "A bad man. He had killed one of his own" (156). As Fools Crow observes, "He had turned away from his own people" (157). Moreover, Owl Child's rejection of his people, as he adopts many of the characteristics of the white men that he so despises, is a rejection of the land as well as its people. Like the stories, the landscape functions ontologically here, as it does in much American Indian literature, according to Robert Nelson (277). Owl Child's marginalization and alienation contrast with Fools Crow's close connection to his people and the land that he remains a part of. It is this sense of connection which creates the powerfully positive potential of *Fools Crow*'s story.

Welch's choice of the Western as the form for his ethnographic/historical novel suggests specific links between the conventions of the formula Western and Blackfeet culture and experience. The physical environment and landscape, in particular, are shaped by this experience. Typically, in Western novels and movies, the Indian is merely part of the landscape. In fact, that landscape is secondary to the white "civilized" people living on it, riding over it, taming it—dominating it. In contrast, the landscape of *Fools Crow* is a living entity. It is a character, speaking to the peoples living *in* it, rather than *on* it. As Nelson observes, "The discovery or invention of the relationship between land and human beings (that is, the process of human identification) drives the 'plot' and becomes the main 'theme' in these works" (271). The landscape constructs another level of dialogue between multidimensional worlds of experience; the separation and opposition between natural and supernatural worlds, the inanimate physical world and the human, no longer hold. This is a conceptual space where mountains and bears can, and do, speak to people. It is a place where mountains, rivers, canyons, and other features of the physical landscape are "more than landmarks" to the Blackfeet (*Fools Crow* 3).

Laurence Evers notes that, "Cultural landscapes are created by the imaginative interaction of societies of men and particular geographies" (244). He states, "By imagining who and what they are in relation to particular landscapes, cultures and individual members of cultures form a close relation with those landscapes" (243). In *Fools Crow*, as in much contemporary American Indian literature, oral tradition is the dominant trope in imagining and organizing the relationship of a people to the landscape. Landscape as the device of fiction is perhaps more prevalent in the Western than in any other genre of fiction. In the Western the land appears as universal archetype; it is a meta-landscape, rather than a regionally specific one. In the formula Western, landmarks resemble absent physical spaces. The hills, the rocks, the desolate plains—all of these could be found anywhere in the apparently uninhabited West of the frontier American imagination. Indians do not populate this landscape except as imagined savages—bloodthirsty or otherwise—of a fantastically white imagination.

The landscape undermines this Western conceptualization in *Fools Crow*. Both Indians and land comprise the foreground, rather than the background context, of cultural experience. Welch's physical environment reveals a sense of locale where place names suggest, as Jane Tompkins notes, "field[s] of action and...fund[s] of sensation" and "lend historicity and romance" to the story (79). However, Welch consistently gives the reader Western scenes where the action is all Indian and where the historicity of the moment is liable to elude mainstream Anglo-American readers. This landscape converges with story and history to reveal a kind of ethnography written as fiction.

Throughout *Fools Crow* the familiar landscape of Montana is defamiliarized; the reader perceives the land in new and culturally unfamiliar ways. Stories are embedded in the land, and the landscape itself is embedded in the history of a people. As the narrator observes, Chief Mountain, "...was more than a landmark to the Pikunis, Kainahs and Siksikas, the three tribes of the Blackfeet, for it was on top of Chief Mountain that the blackhorn skull pillows of the great warriors still lay" (3). This is the place where Morning Star and Star Boy return to earth each morning to see Feather Woman (*Fools Crow* 350–52). To construct meaning from out of this text, the reader must interpret Blackfeet experience of the Black Hills. These Black Hills of Chief Mountain are not the same hills of the Western frontier imagination. While the non-Native reader struggles to make sense of this new vision of the physical environment, a Blackfeet reader would recognize a familiar landscape written into the unfamiliar context of a novel. The simultaneous defamiliarization and invocation of the landscape, and its ability to generate meaning in multiple ways, transforms the lay of the land into something beyond mere physical presence.

Welch's interpretation of the Blackfeet landscape works to collapse literary genre and historical events with physical space and real people, constructing a text or narration where the West is no longer a historicized fiction or a fictionalized history. While Davidson observes that, "The West always was a state of mind and a state of history rather than a specific geographical location" (141), that is clearly not the case in *Fools Crow* and, I would argue, much American Indian writing. Even the traditional names of places suggest stories—names like Backbone of the World, Woman Don't Walk Butte, Red Old Man's Butte, and Always Summer Land. These are stories that many of us have not heard or read. The names do more, however, than suggest a quaint Indian-ness. They contribute to the sense of the landscape as living and interacting with the people that remain a part of it. They hint at an intimacy and interrelationship with the land that is missing from white accounts of the same country.

Differences between Indian and white interpretations of the same landscape are highlighted when the narrator describes the effect of the land on the white wagoner. These are the Mountains of the Backbone through which Raven had previously led White Man's Dog, giving him the magic of Skunk Bear (*Fools Crow* 55), and where Fools Crow has his visions of a desolate future where, "It was as if the earth had swallowed up the animals …. To see such a vast, empty prairie made Fools Crow uneasy" (356). Fools Crow's new unease mirrors white experience of the land. The white wagoner finds that, "The rolling prairies were as vast and empty as a pale ocean…. The few small groups of mountains…only seemed to emphasize its vastness" (289–90). Or, as another white rider puts it, "What a hell of a country" (242). This sense of isolation and alienation from the physical world, Welch implies, is a white dis-ease.

While the descriptions of the anonymous white characters contrast vividly with Fools Crow's Blackfeet experience, they are what one would expect in a Western where, as Tompkins states, the message is, "Come, and suffer." Here, "Everything [including humanity] blends imperceptibly into the desert" (Tompkins 72). The Indians of *Fools Crow* suffer as much as any cowboy. Even so, their suffering is part of the suffering of the land. Moreover, historical trivialization and ignorance of such suffering mirrors the many indignities imposed on the physical environment by gold miners, farmers, and now tourists. Today, the sacred hills of the Blackfeet remain home to, as Welch aptly describes it, "all kinds of silliness" in its many tourist attractions (*Killing Custer* 78).

The defamiliarization of the fictive landscape of the West encourages a reading of *Fools Crow* as more than simply fiction and more than history. It may be read as "autoethnography," where, as Mary Louise Pratt states, "Colonized subjects…represent themselves in ways that *engage with* the colonizer's own terms" (7). Autoethnography arises through the process of transculturation, Pratt argues. Marginalized groups select and *invent from* materials drawn from dominant culture (Pratt 6; emphasis mine). Pratt makes the distinction between engaging with and reproducing Western discourse. One could argue that Welch does not reproduce the discourse of the formula cowboy and Indian Western or the discourse of European literary tradition: he engages with both to reveal that the difference between Blackfeet oral tradition and Western written tradition is ultimately not an essential one. In Fools Crow's final vision, he feels "a happiness that sleeps with sadness" (390). Such contradictory feelings remain a sign of the times. *Fools Crow* reveals place as memory, story, and history; the trajectory of these three intersects with readings of resistance and Pratt's notion of autoethnography. This becomes clear in *Killing Custer*, where Welch writes a "factual" rather than a fictive Indian history of the battle at Little Bighorn and the earlier Marias River Massacre. As Welch searches out the exact location of the Marias River Massacre, a location "lost" to history and which Welch, with difficulty, "found," and re-located, it becomes apparent that place *remains* tied to story and history—and resistance—right into the present. In *Killing Custer*, as in *Fools Crow*, Welch links the personal with the historical. Getting the place, as well as the story, right, is crucial.

Ultimately, *Fools Crow* suggests a way of understanding disconnections, as well as connections, between two distinct worldviews. As Heavy Shield Woman listens to the story of Star Woman and connects her experience of the world back to the origins of the sacred Sun ceremony, the reader becomes immersed in the Blackfeet world of Fools Crow. Furthermore, the reader confronts the history lying behind the novel as fiction. The meaning of the stories, and the larger "story" of the novel itself, is perhaps more important than some of the events themselves. The reader makes connections between different stories. For the most part, however, there are disconnections between the story of Fools Crow and the history of the white reader. Those disconnections, I suggest, begin with language and lead towards a particular sense of the landscape and the land as an integral part of Blackfeet culture. They culminate in a new sense of what comprises the Native American Indian novel.

The connection between the American Indian and the landscape is a connection between place and story; this connection provides one with knowledge of how to live in the world. This knowledge, as Keith Basso observes, "Focus[es] as much on *where* events occurred as on the nature and consequences of the events themselves.... Narrated events are *spatially anchored*" (26). It is finally the absence of an anchored white perspective in *Fools Crow* that becomes ominously present. By engaging with white perceptions of the landscape, but simultaneously insisting on the primacy of Blackfeet experience and interpretation, the whites, in Welch's story, are dis-placed. This displacement allows for a positive reading of the end of the novel. *Fools Crow*, among other things, may therefore be read as a site of cultural resistance.

The American Indian novel has constructed something new. The landscape of *Fools Crow* and other American Indian texts reinforces Davidson's claim that these books share, "A borderlands model of the West as a wavering and elusive site of hybridity, cross-fertilization, complication, and ideological contestation and transformation (as opposed to manifest certainty)" (36). This ideological contestation of, among other things, the landscape, leads to a reading of American Indian novels as sites of cultural resistance. As Edward Said notes, the novel form, instead of preventing another sort of narrative from "forming and emerging" in true colonial style (xiii) may be used and transformed by authors to "assert their own identity and the existence of their own history" (Said xii). American Indian authors like James Welch are transforming the way their histories and identities are being read and constructed. Novels like *Fools Crow* recuperate specific notions of cultural identity and link identity with notions of literary genre and critiques of ideology. Read as, among other things, a study in genre, *Fools Crow* concerns itself with ideological issues surrounding the representation of "Indianness." Ultimately, *Fools Crow* is both novel and history, fact and fiction, ethnographic and literary. If form and content are finally intimate and inseparable, then form in conjunction with content makes this genre novel. In a tradition where dreams empower individuals in real, physical, and tangible ways, perhaps novels like this may be able to do the same thing. Perhaps they are like dreams.

Notes

1. See James Welch's book, *Killing Custer*, for a detailed discussion of the events leading up to this massacre, as well as its connection to the Battle at Little Bighorn.

2. Robinson stresses this point repeatedly on the taped recordings of his stories, during his ten years of discussions and storytelling with ethnographer Wendy Wickwire.

3. Robin Ridington pointed out this feature of oral stories to me during personal communication in March of 1997.

4. This was pointed out to me in conversation with Robin Ridington in March of 1997.

Works Cited

Basso, Keith H. "'Stalking with Stories': Names, Places, and Moral Narrative Among the Western Apache." *Text, Play and Story: Proceedings of the AES*. Washington: American Anthropological Association, 1984. 19–55.

Dasenbrock, Reed Way. "Intelligibility and Meaningfulness in Multicultural Literature in English." *Academic Reading*. Ed. Janet Giltrow. Peterborough: Broadview Press, 1995. 305–24.

Davidson, Arnold E. *Coyote Country: Fictions of the Canadian West*. Durham: Duke U P, 1994.

Evers, Laurence J. "Words and Place: A Reading of [N. Scott Momaday's] *House Made of Dawn*." *Critical Essays on the Western American Novel*. Ed. William T. Pilkington. Boston: G.K. Hall & Co., 1980. 243–61.

Francis, Daniel. *The Imaginary Indian: The Image of the Indian in Canadian Culture*. Vancouver: Arsenal Pulp Press, 1992.

Grinnell, George Bird. *Blackfoot Lodge Tales*. Lincoln: U of Nebraska P, 1962.

Irwin, Lee. *The Dream Seekers: Native American Visionary Traditions of the Great Plains*. Norman: U of Oklahoma P, 1994.

Momaday, N. Scott. "Personal Reflections." *The American Indian and the Problem of History*. Ed. Calvin Martin. New York: Oxford U P, 1987. 156–62.

Nelson, Robert M.   "Place, Vision, and Identity in Native American Literatures." *American Indian Studies: An Interdisciplinary Approach to Contemporary Issues*. Ed. Dane Morrison. New York: Peter Lang, 1997. 265–85.

Owens, Louis. *Other Destinies: Understanding the American Indian Novel*. Norman: U of Oklahoma P, 1992.

Pratt, Mary Louise. *Imperial Eyes: Travel Writing and Transculturation*. London: Routledge, 1992.

Robinson, Harry. *Nature Power*. Vancouver: Douglas & McIntyre, 1992.

Robinson, Harry. *Write It on Your Heart*. Vancouver: Talonbooks, 1989.

Said, Edward W. *Culture and Imperialism*. New York: Alfred A. Knopf, 1993.

Sarris, Greg.   *Keeping Slug Woman Alive: A Holistic Approach to American Indian Texts*. Berkeley: U of California P, 1993.

Tompkins, Jane P. *West of Everything: The Inner Life of Westerns*. New York: Oxford U P, 1992.

Welch, James. *Fools Crow*. New York: Penguin, 1986.

Welch, James. *Killing Custer*. New York: W.W. Norton Company, 1994.

Welch, James. *Winter in the Blood*. New York: Penguin, 1974.

Wiebe, Rudy. *The Scorched Wood People*. Toronto: McClelland and Stewart, 1977.

Wiebe, Rudy. *The Temptations of Big Bear*. Toronto: McClelland and Stewart, 1973.

10

Native American Sleuths: Following in the Footsteps of the Indian Guides?

John K. Donaldson

The past two decades have seen a proliferation of mystery novels in which Native Americans play the part of police detective, private investigator, or amateur sleuth. Tony Hillerman is by far the best known of the authors involved in this trend. In fact, his works are generally regarded as the standard by which all others in the new subgenre are measured, not only because he is its probable creator, but also because of his mastery of the form.[1] Joining forces with Hillerman's Navajo policemen, Officer Jim Chee and Lieutenant Joe Leaphorn, we now have Native American sleuths of both genders representing a wide variety of tribes. There are Peter Bowen's amateur (and somewhat unwilling) Métis detective, Gabriel Du Pré; James Doss's Ute policeman, Charlie Moon; Jean Hager's Cherokee investigator, Molly Bearpaw, and police chief, Joe Bushyhead; Thomas Perry's free-lance operative, Jane Whitefield, a Seneca; and David and Aimée Thurlo's FBI agent, turned tribal police officer, Ella Clah, another Navajo, to name the most prominent among them.[2]

Authenticity in Texts Authored by Whites

Apart from the successful rendering of these characters as literary creations and aside from their relative skills at detection, the question of their "Indianness" arises. At one point in Thomas Perry's novel *Vanishing Act* (1995), Jane Whitefield exclaims, "I'm as Indian as I can be!" But is this completely accurate, and would it hold true of the other supposedly Native American protagonists of popular contemporary mystery and suspense novels? Or, is their attributed ethnicity merely an excuse for the introduction of "atmosphere" and "color," whether authentic or not? Are they simply modernized versions of the Indian scouts and trusty guides of earlier periods of American fiction—starting with the Leatherstocking Tales? Given the traditions established by both literature and cinema in the U.S., one might easily expect a modern-day Uncas or Chingachgook, or a Tonto—a sidekick *cum* straight man—playing Watson to some white Sherlock. There is also the possibility that in acts of over-correction for past negative stereotypes, Native American protagonists may be presented with magnified virtues and exaggerated prowess, reviving in new guise the myth of the noble savage—which is also a stereotype and therefore also dehumanizing.

Happily, these concerns mostly turn out to be unfounded, and, to the extent to which they materialize, the error is more often in the direction of glorification than denigration. For example, Thomas Perry's tough, independent P.I., Jane Whitefield, expert in the martial arts and mistress of disguise, seems to have more in common with V. I. Warshawski,[3] than with the ethnological profile of a Seneca woman. Whitefield, however, can operate in both worlds, mainstream and Indian, and when moving among her fellow Senecas, her speech, her demeanor, her behavior in general are modified so as to put her in touch and keep her in step with her fellow tribesmen. Moreover, the Seneca background—both contemporary and historical—is handled with accuracy and understanding.

Jennifer Talldeer, the part-Osage, part-Cherokee heroine created by Mercedes Lackey for her novel *Sacred Ground* (1994), is likewise at times too good to be true. In addition to being a private investigator, she is an apprentice shaman, and makes use of her supernatural powers in her detective work. This is a clever idea for purposes of both plotting and characterization; even so, it needs to be handled with the greatest subtlety and dexterity. Otherwise, new clichés—the Indian as repository of both natural and supernatural wisdom, for instance—take the place of old ones. Furthermore, clairvoyance and teleperception, as devices, risk pushing the novel over the dividing line between detective and supernatural fiction. When Jennifer flies (and not by airplane) we are definitely on the other side of that boundary. However, the bits of Osage and Cherokee history and lore incorporated into the fabric of the novel display respect and a concern for accuracy.

Similarly, in *Blackening Song* (1995) where the Thurlos' creation, Ella

Clah, made her debut, there is an over-reliance on the supernatural as a device to further the action. However, by the time of Ella's second and third appearances, in *Death Walker* (1996) and *Bad Medicine* (1997), supernatural elements, while still present, are handled much more deftly. Again, there is every reason to believe that great effort was made to insure reasonable accuracy in regard to the elements of Navajo culture that are included. It must be remembered that, in the Native American view, respectful treatment of their traditions, especially in regard to the supernatural, calls for strategic omissions and minor alterations—changes that do not affect the general spirit, tone, or "feel" of the particular belief or practice being described, but are sufficient to safeguard its integrity and conceal its true identity from outsiders.

Texts with Supernatural Elements

The inclusion of supernatural elements in detective fiction with Indian characters is a complex problem. Traditional Amerindian worldview does not make a natural/supernatural distinction, but western literary traditions do. The novel of the supernatural or the occult has generic properties different from those of both the detective and the espionage novel. Authenticity in characterization and background would therefore argue for inclusion of supernatural elements, while generic restraints, particularly as they apply to plotting, militate against it. Nevertheless, when handled carefully, it seems possible to infuse detective fiction with paranormal ingredients if certain restrictions are observed: The supernatural should never dominate; it should never be the main ingredient; it should never be the sole element advancing the plot; and, most certainly, it should never be the means of resolving the essential problem or puzzle at the heart of the narrative. It should be closely linked, in some fashion, to the character or background of one (or more) of the major personages. Finally, it should reflect actual Native American beliefs and attitudes and not the fertility of the author's imagination.

Perhaps the best example of a successful use of the supernatural on a small scale is in the James Doss novels, where Daisy Perika, the traditionalist aunt of Ute detective, Charlie Moon, attains insights into crimes (before and after they have been committed) through paranormal means. This, however, seems thoroughly appropriate since she is a shaman. By making her revelations part of her belief system, rather than asking the reader to alter his or her own beliefs (or to suspend disbelief), Doss simultaneously furthers the development of Daisy's portrayal and introduces a supernatural element. He presents us with a realistic portrayal of what is unreal (from our point of view) by making it a dimension of character and culture. The fact that her nephew is skeptical of Daisy's visions also helps to keep the supernatural element from overwhelming the plot, while, at the same time, allowing it to contribute to the novel's atmosphere. In this way, verisimilitude is successfully joined to verity.

An outstanding use of the supernatural on a larger scale (i.e., related to the plot of the novel as a whole, its main theme, and main character) is to be found in Muriel Gray's 1995 work, *The Trickster*. Clearly drawing upon Northern versions of the pan-Indian Trickster myth (which tend to be more sinister and more mysterious than their Southern counterparts) and interpreting them with a rationalist European sensibility, which inclines to view the supernatural as monstrous, Gray produces a combined horror/crime novel in which the protagonist is an Indian who has rejected—indeed denied—his heritage. The solution of the mystery, the termination of the horror, the safety of his family, the welfare of the community, and his own mental health all depend on his rediscovering and accepting his identity and reclaiming a belief system that includes the supernatural—in other words, admitting a view of the world in which the occult is a real presence, and in which there are, therefore, valid ways to approach and deal with it.

Although the supernatural plays a role in several of Jean Hagar's Cherokee mysteries, it is subordinated to character and plot, rather than dominating them.[4] If one is to find fault with the use of the Cherokee belief system—or Cherokee culture in general—in her novels, it would be that perhaps she does not explore deeply enough. That is to say, Cherokee lore sometimes remains peripheral to both the mystery and its solution—adding local color to the Oklahoma setting, but not really essential. However, in the more satisfying novels in her Cherokee series, the Indian elements are fully integrated and are crucial to both the questions posed and answers given. And, in all cases, the Cherokee material is approached respectfully, in a way that never leaves the reader in doubt as to whether the author has done her homework. An additional criticism, nonetheless, might be that Hager draws upon contemporary Western Cherokee folk practices without sufficient reference to the complex traditional belief system of which they are but a reflection. That, however, may well indicate the state of her informants' knowledge of their own culture in present-day Oklahoma.

Commonalities in Native American Mystery Texts

If the major practitioners of this new genre have, by and large, avoided the chief pitfalls one might have anticipated they would tumble into, the next question is whether any dominant tendencies have emerged in their writing and whether one may gain any useful insights into the reasons behind its successful execution. Obviously, one wonders also about the reasons for the enormously enthusiastic public acceptance of the subgenre, as well as about the craftsmanship of the authors involved. The answers to these questions seem to be closely related.

It has often been pointed out that the classic mystery story presupposes an ordered universe, one in which cause and effect are operative, one where both inductive and deductive logic are able to function, and one in which there exists an underlying truth. Therein, lies the mystery story's basic distinction from the espionage novel, which, by contrast, assumes a chaotic world where deception prevails. Although traditional American Indian belief systems do not validate Western forms of logic and linear, cause-and-effect modes of thought, they do entail a conception of reality in which everything is interrelated to everything else in a state of universal harmony or balance. A disturbance of that balance calls human beings into action, first to discover the source of the imbalance and then to correct it. Therefore, in a strange way, the work of the classic detective character in the face of a crime parallels the task of any traditional Native American working within his or her own belief system in the presence of a disequilibrium (that is to say, in our terms, a crime or catastrophe).

Peter Freese, in a chapter in *American Popular Culture at Home and Abroad* (1996), has examined this strange parallel between the universe of the mystery story and that of traditional Native American philosophy at great length. His exploration mostly limits itself to the work of Tony Hillerman, but it is applicable to all the mysteries in which Native

American sleuths dig for clues, hunt the guilty, search out explanations. Freese contends that the Native American detective, an Indian with a mainstream occupation—and one that has a long, distinguished tradition of literary representation—becomes *ipso facto* a mediator between dominant and Indian culture. This observation leads us back full circle to the initial question of whether or not the Indian detectives so prevalent in today's American mystery fiction, represent a new form of literary exploitation by being nothing more than variations on old stereotypes of the Indian guides, pathfinders, and interpreters.

In Euro-American literature, there is a convention of "good Indians" (that is to say, Indians who help whites do whatever it is whites want to do) being regarded as "cultural mediators." Mixed-blood characters have often been cast in the same role. This is also a part that contemporary mixed-blood writers have been expected to play (as, for example, W. S. Penn admonishes in *All My Sins Are Relatives*, 1995) or denigrated for performing (as in Paul Zolbrod's remarks about contemporary Native American poets: that they are all products of creative writing courses and mixbloods to boot—with the implication that by those tokens they are doubly lacking in authenticity) (1995, 91).

Texts Authored by Native Americans

In this connection, it is noteworthy that, with a few important exceptions, the authors of major detective fiction with Native American protagonists are not themselves Indian, full or mixed-blood. Sherman Alexie has written a crime novel (*Indian Killer*, 1996) and the detective in it lays claim to being Indian, but isn't really, whereas the major suspects are. Louis Owens (in *The Sharpest Sight*, 1992) has used the framework of the mystery novel, but transformed it into something quite different. Moreover, his detective is a Chicano, technically part Indian if his bloodline were to be traced back far enough, but one who identifies with Hispanic, not Native American culture. Many of the same characters reappear in Owens's next novel, *Bone Game* (1994). By this juncture, the direction in which Owens is taking the genre becomes clearer, for in *Bone Game* it can be said that the events happen to the characters, who solve the mystery by remaining strangely passive, allowing it unfold itself. This tendency is even more evident in Owens's next novel, *Nightland* (1996). In A. A. Carr's *Eye Killers* (1995), the amateur sleuth is a white woman—although she is aided by several elderly Navajos. Furthermore, *Eye Killers* is a vampire novel and mainly follows the conventions of that genre.

Turning to less well known Indian or part-Indian writers, one sees that either they produce variants rather than classic mystery novels, or that their fictive detective is not a Native American, or that their focus is not on Indian characters and settings. William Sanders, for example, has created a mystery series set in Oklahoma, but his detective, Taggart Roper, is a white man. Roper happens to have a Cherokee girlfriend; however, only one novel in this series, *Blood Autumn* (1996), is primarily about Indians. *The Tree People* (1995) by Naomi Stokes does contain a Native American law enforcement officer, Jordan Tidewater, who is the first woman to be sheriff of her Northwest Coast reservation. Jordan, however, does not really solve the mystery and supernatural elements might be said to dominate the plot.

The chief exception to the general rule that Native American sleuths are the creations of white authors is Martin Cruz Smith, best known for his Russian detective in such novels as *Gorky Park* (1981), or, most recently, his Lancashire investigator in *Rose* (1996). Smith's early work, *Nightwing* (1977) did, however, feature a Hopi police deputy, Youngman Duran. The fruit of Duran's detection, on the other hand, was to uncover a natural disaster, rather than a crime; this circumstance arguably moves that novel into a different generic category. A later work, *Stallion Gate* (1986), featuring a Native American investigator, has elements of both historical and espionage fiction. Therefore, it, too, may be considered as not belonging to the detective genre. Furthermore, the protagonist, Sergeant Joe Peña, constantly runs counter to the role he has been assigned and subverts the investigation he is involved in. In the light of these facts, Smith's works may not really be the exceptions they initially seemed.

The Tay-bodal series by Mardi Oakley Medawar constitutes another possible exception. Medawar has developed the persona of a Kiowa healer (Tay-bodal) who utilizes keen observation and both inductive and deductive reasoning to trace illnesses back to their causes. His Holmesian blend of perception and cerebration are on occasion applied to unearthing the motives behind crimes and thus uncovering the perpetrators. However, the two stories in which Tay-bodal appears, *Death at Rainy Mountain* (1996) and *Witch of the Palo Duro* (1997), are also historical novels with a nineteenth-century Kiowa setting. Consequently, since whites figure only peripherally in them, these works do not present the kind of inter-character dialogue that serves the mediational function for the reader observed in other novels with Native American sleuths. Nonetheless, it could be argued that the author sets up an intellectual (and perhaps even emotional) dialogue between the novel, its setting, characters, and events, on the one hand, and the reader's expectations, on the other.

Mediation and Dialogue in Texts

If, then, the new contingent of Indian detectives who have appeared on the scene in the last decade are mainly the creations of whites, the question of the stereotyping of a minority group by representatives of the majority society is once again raised. On examination, it can be said that the new Native American detectives do indeed act as mediators, but that they are far from stereotypical ones. There are two principal factors rescuing them from that fate. First, the authors' knowledge of the various cultures they describe is seemingly greater than that of many writers in the past. All of them have been in contact with the tribal groups and the areas they describe. All of them have obviously done research. Accompanying this greater knowledge, what can best be termed a respectful (positive, but not idealized or reverential) attitude toward the culture is evidenced. With a more accurate fund of knowledge comes recognition that within Amerindian cultures—as is true of any ethnic group—there are a variety of personality types acting upon different motivations, in accordance with a range of beliefs. This more complex view of the Indian in his own culture goes hand in hand with—indeed, makes possible—the second factor that aids in averting stereotypes: The mediation the main characters perform is carried out in concert with other Indian characters through some kind of social interaction or dialogue—most frequently between members of the same family. Since Native American belief systems emphasize the interrelatedness of all reality, including all people, this is indeed an appropriate device. Moreover, kinship-based models are characteristic paradigms in Native American thought (Sahlins 1976, 211–12; Salisbury 1987, 50).

The character groupings, which can involve numerous individuals, are usually composed of "traditionalist" in opposition to "progressive" or "assimilationist." This diversity allows the portrayal of a broader spectrum of contemporary Indian attitudes. It also provides space for a great deal of humor. As one character becomes a comic foil for another, or, as roles are reversed, expectations of both the other characters and the reader are surprised. An example of the irony that the multiple-character device allows is to be found in the relationship between Jim Chee and Joe Leaphorn in the Hillerman novels. Contrary to expectations and therefore militating against the creation of type, it is the youthful Chee who is the traditionalist and the elder Leaphorn (who, among other things has studied ethnography) who represents the progressive. At the same time, Chee's part-Navajo girlfriend, Janet Pete, a successful lawyer who has worked with a prominent Washington firm, is a force pulling him away from the reservation and the traditional life, while Leaphorn's white lady friend, Professor Louisa Bourebonette, an anthropologist, is comfortable with the ways of both Navajo and mainstream society.

In all three of James Doss's novels (*The Shaman Sings*, 1994, *The Shaman Laughs*, 1995, and *The Shaman's Bones*, 1997), circumstances bring the white policeman, Scott Parris to the Southern Ute reservation where protocol demands that he work with tribal police officer, Charlie Moon. In the course of their joint investigations, Moon has numerous occasions to explain Ute ways to Parris. However, the real foil for Charlie Moon is not the white man, Parris, but his elderly aunt, the shaman, Daisy Parika, whose wisdom, perceptiveness, deeper knowledge of Ute culture, and closer contact with both the natural and spiritual worlds lead her to solve the mysteries long before her modern, professionally-trained nephew stumbles across the solution or accidentally bumps into the perpetrator. The Charlie Moon-Daisy Perika contrast is of the type most frequently found in current detective fiction featuring Native Americans. It involves cerebration, linear cause-and-effect reasoning, scientific methodology, weighing of probabilities, and compulsive or "driven" action, on the one hand, versus a state of being more in tune with, more receptive to one's surroundings, more in contact with the natural world (which, in the framework of traditional Native American thought, includes also human nature and what we would call the supernatural). Doss makes clear that sensitivity to extrasensory stimuli is a personal, psychological trait as well as a culturally conditioned one by characterizing the white man, Scott Parris, as more receptive to Daisy's revelations than her own blood relation, Charlie Moon. Indeed, Scott seems to be subject to paranormal experiences himself, although he tries his best to rationalize them.

The other significant aspect of the character alignment Doss gives us is that it entails a three-way contrast. In this case, it is traditional Indian/acculturated Indian/sympathetic white. This schema is typical of much of the subgenre of detective fiction with Native American sleuths. Looking back at the Hillerman novels as a whole with this in mind, we see, in effect, a double triangle: Leaphorn-Chee-Pete, and Chee-Leaphorn-Bourebonette, or, partially-acculturated Indian/traditionalist Indian/fully-acculturated part-Indian and traditionalist Indian/partially-acculturated Indian/sympathetic white, respectively.

A triangular relationship also exists in Mercedes Lackey's *Sacred Ground* (1994). Jennifer Talldeer is by profession a private investigator and by avocation an apprentice shaman under the tutelage of her grandfather, Frank. We have in their relationship a recapitulation of the story of many American minorities vis-à-vis the mainstream. The children have—at least partially—rejected their heritage, but the grandchildren are attracted by it. However, not having acquired their traditions through unbroken generational transmission, they must regain them at a later age, and in a somewhat formalized manner from grandparents, teachers, tribal elders. The third point in the Jennifer/Frank Talldeer triangle is occupied by David Spotted Horse, Jennifer's sometime boyfriend, an activist, who challenges her apolitical and insufficiently traditional behavior.

In the first of the Thurlo novels, *Blackening Song* (1995), Ella Clah is part of a four-way relationship. On the Anglo side is the competitive, insensitive, blundering, duplicitous FBI agent with whom she must work to solve the crime of her own father's murder—"must" because the crime occurred on an Indian reservation over which the Federal Government and its agencies have jurisdiction. Ella boasts to him and to others of her professionalism, her training in the scientific methodology of detection, but, as far as the reader can perceive, she never gets anywhere on her own in solving the crime. Like Charlie Moon, she blunders her way along. It is her brother, a shaman, and her mother, each possessing a wealth of tribal knowledge as well as keenly honed perceptions, who constantly keep heading her in the right directions. Yet, as they repeatedly point out, she has the same innate discernment as they, the same insights and intuitions. She, however, disregards these attributes—indeed stifles them by refusing to develop them or even to recognize their validity. In other words, it is as if her professional training had, ironically, undone her natural resources of insightfulness, perceptiveness, intuitiveness, and thus rendered her less, rather than more fit for her job. The strong implication is that the two approaches to detection, the two sets of skills, those associated with Indian and those associated with white culture, should be complementary, rather than one supplanting the other. However, if only one is to prevail, the Indian mode is clearly far more valuable, at least when working with Indians in their own cultural context, on their home ground.

By the time of Ella's third appearance, in *Bad Medicine* (1997), she has attained greater psychological equilibrium (having recovered from the double trauma of the death of her husband and a bloody shoot-out she was involved in) and she has also achieved a better balance between causal analysis and extrasensory perception as ways of knowing. Truly confident in herself, she is less prone to braggadocio. Her relations with her mother and brother are smoother, and she even communicates better with her fractious FBI counterpart, Blalock, who reciprocates by being more considerate of Navajo sensibilities. Mediation has taken place among the characters as well as on behalf of the reader.

The ostensible four-way relationship in the Ella Clah novels is really just a variation on the characteristic triangle of the subgenre. Ella's mother and brother represent different but related aspects of traditional Navajo culture. That these elements are divided between two characters betokens their complexity and also the traditional male/female associations of many roles in Navajo culture.

In Peter Bowen's so-called "Montana Novels,"[5] the Métis sleuth, Gabriel Du Pré is frequently in dialogue with his rich white friend and neighbor, Bart Fascelli, and the aged and impoverished traditionalist, Benetsee (who, in addition, happens to be a seer.) Even more important, however, is the dialogue Du Pré holds with himself as he debates moral, political, social issues from the points of view of modern American, as opposed to traditional Métis culture. The different sides of Du Pré's character, which alternately conflict with each other and resolve into determined action, perform the function of mediation for the reader.

Texts That Turn Tables

In the overview, the relationships portrayed in almost all the novels in the subgenre present us with some important reversals: First of all, ancient and arcane knowledge rivals and often outdoes modern science. Too bad the two can't recognize each other's worth and work together is the implication. Second, amateurs who know the people they are working with and the total cultural context with which they are dealing can outperform professionals. Third, Indians who have turned their backs on their cultural heritage or are simply ignorant about it or indifferent to it have little more competence in solving mysteries when they occur among other Indians than do outsiders.   Thomas Perry's novels, however, turn the tables in an altogether different way. Jane Whitefield, his protagonist, is a sleuth in reverse, involved in creating mysteries as much as solving them. Instead of uncovering guilty parties, she is chiefly committed to hiding innocent ones who are in danger, hence the title of the first novel in the series, *Vanishing Act* (1995). She refers to herself as a "guide," and indeed she is a kind of Sacajawea or Malinche—with a difference. She leads white people out of the white world and into the Indian one, not as conquerors and dispossessors, but as refugees seeking asylum. These are defeated white people running from the cruelest, most depraved aspects of modern society: abused wives and children fleeing abusive husbands and fathers, targets of organized crime, intended murder victims. The world they are escaping is hideously reminiscent of the one portrayed by Native American writer, Leslie Marmon Silko in *Almanac of the Dead* (1991). Sometimes Jane hides these individuals on Indian reservations. In the deepest irony, it is on the reservation, in an entire society that has been abused, that some of these abused individuals find healing through interconnectedness. Perry's second novel, *Dance for the Dead* (1996) ends with one of these white refugees participating in the Seneca Dance for the Dead (hence the book's name). This is a ceremony of healing as well as of memory and mourning.

In addition to being a guide, Jane is also an interpreter—an interpreter of traditional Seneca ways for the modern, non-Seneca reader. She does this through interactions and conversations with her fellow Indians and by her visits to reservations and to other sites important to Seneca history and culture. The passages describing Seneca rituals bring them alive for the reader in a way that ethnographic description rarely does. The most recent novel in which Jane appears, *Shadow Woman* (1997), is more psychological in its focus, concentrating on the workings of not only Jane's mind, but those of the criminals and their intended victims. Nevertheless, the visit to the reservation and the reenactment of ancient rituals are still important to the plot and to Jane's characterization. In one passage Jane's recall of a bit of Iroquois folklore saves her life and that of the man she is protecting. In *Shadow Woman*, as in each of its predecessors, there is a moment when Jane, standing on some spot significant in Seneca history, re-envisions the events which took place there. These passages are invariably beautifully crafted—delicate, although they contain violent actions; poignant, because they are windows offering glimpses of a once-living culture, now gone forever; and disturbing because they reveal the whites' role in ending that way of life.

The Function of Native American Mystery Texts in Popular Culture

The characteristics that Perry evidences in these passages—the detailed and accurate knowledge of a minority group's culture; an attitude which is not only sympathetic, but respectful of that culture; sensitivity toward the feelings of group members—these are some of the qualities that set the whole group of Native American detective novels apart from their predecessors, the stories of Indian guides and interpreters, who, in terms of plot, were but convenient instruments to the execution of the white man's will, and in terms of audience, but a means of entertainment and diversion in their "exoticism." One factor contributing to this transformation may be a literary discontinuity. Hillerman claims to have been influenced, not by his American literary antecedents, but by the Australian detective stories of Arthur Upfield (Holt 1980, 6; Freese 1996, 105). In a series of twenty-nine novels, Upfield's creation, Detective Inspector Napoleon Bonaparte of the Queensland Police, son of a white father and an Aborigine mother, equipped with a Brisbane University M.A. and a store of tribal lore, solves crimes using the knowledge and the modes of reasoning he has acquired from both sources.[6] "Boney," as he is nicknamed, constantly faces down prejudice by asserting his own dignity and demonstrating his considerable talents. One would like to think that the American literary scene was ripe for the introduction of fictional characters shaped in Boney's mold as we move to a more truly multicultural society. In such a society, members of the mainstream demonstrate a sincere desire to know more about and to respect members of minority groups. This new attitude might help explain the fact that Hillerman and the writers who followed his lead readily carved out for themselves such a solid literary niche. In doing so they have helped make the most "American" elements conceivable—the lives and cultures of the First Americans—more familiar to the mainstream, rather than exploiting them for the sake of purveying a bogus exoticism.

It is certainly true that mystery fans thirst for atmosphere, and, like tourists are always looking for new "terrain" to explore. More importantly, however, throughout our nation's history, Americans have used literature as a medium to search out and validate their roots. Often this has meant spiritual returns to Europe, Africa, Asia. Some authors, on the other hand, have tried to put down roots on American soil. This has frequently meant exploring the relationship with the natural environment. At other times it has meant establishing links with Native American culture. Willa Cather's work, a case in point, offers outstanding examples of both these latter tendencies, e.g., *The Professor's House* (1925) or *The Song of the Lark* (1915). It is in this tradition of exploring our national unity, our ties to each other, our connection with the land, our links to a common past that the new novels with Native American sleuths belong, rather than in the now outworn Cooperesque tradition of the Indian sidekick. For the inaccurately drawn, stereotyped, but exotic Indians of another era, the new genre offers us individualized, fully human representatives of the numerous and diverse Native American cultures that are still a living part of our multiethnic society.

Notes

1. There are now twelve novels in Hillerman's Navajo detective series. They are, in order of their publication: *Blessing Way* (1970), *Dance Hall of the Dead* (1973), *Listening Woman* (1978), *People of Darkness* (1980), *The Dark Wind* (1982), *Ghostway* (1984), *Skinwalkers* (1986), *A Thief of Time* (1988), *Talking God* (1989), *Coyote Waits* (1990), *Sacred Clowns* (1993), *Fallen Man* (1996).

2. This list is not complete. It includes only the best known of those U.S. authors who have produced a "series" of detective stories featuring American Indian sleuths. (Mention of individual novels with Indian crime solvers is found elsewhere in this essay in conjunction with the themes or characteristics they illustrate.) The criterion that an Indian must be the central personage and the one who solves the mystery unfortunately leads to the exclusion of Margaret Coel's *Eagle Catcher* (1995), *Ghost Walker* (1996), and *Dream Stalker* (1997), three very fine works set among the Wind River Arapahos. In these novels, the amateur sleuth is a missionary priest on the reservation. He receives assistance from members of the tribe and is aided by his own sympathetic understanding of their culture. The Father Mark Townsend mysteries by Brad Reynolds, S.J., are excluded for a similar reason. One of these, *A Ritual Death* (1997), is set among Northwest Coast Indians, while the other, *The Story Knife* (1996), takes place among the Yup'ik.

    Even more arbitrarily, Dana Stabenow's excellent Kate Shugak series is not considered solely because Kate is Aleut, not Indian. There are currently a half dozen novels in this entertaining group of mysteries, *A Cold Day for a Murder* (1992), *A Fatal Thaw* (1992), *Dead in the Water* (1993), *A Cold-Blooded Business* (1994), *Blood Will Tell* (1996), and *Breakup* (1997). The widely read and highly regarded mysteries by Canadian novelist Scott Young with their Inuit investigator are not covered for similar reasons. Young has given us two fine novels portraying modern Inuit life, *Murder in a Cold Climate* (1989) and *The Shaman's Knife* (1993).

3. To many mystery fans, Sara Paretsky's creation, V. I. Warshawski, epitomizes the new breed of "tough-gal" detectives. Warshawski appears in several novels, including, for example, *Tunnel Vision* (1994). She is indeed tough-talking, tough-acting, but these characteristics are counterbalanced by her equally tender heart. The same might be said of Jane Whitefield.

4.   There are now eight mysteries by Jean Hager featuring Oklahoma Cherokee detectives. Chief Mitchell Bushyhead figures in *The Grandfather Medicine* (1989), *Night Walker* (1990), *Ghostland* (1992), and *The Fire Carrier* (1996), while Molly Bearpaw is the main character in *Ravenmocker* (1992), *The Redbird's Cry* (1994), *Seven Black Stones* (1995), and *Spirit Catcher* (1997).

5.   Presently, there are four novels in this series: *Coyote Wind* (1994), *Specimen Song* (1995), *Wolf, No Wolf* (1996), and *Notches* (1997).

6.   Perhaps the best-known of Upfield's Australian detective stories in the United States is *The Bone Is Pointed* (1947), which was chosen as a book club selection and later reprinted (1976) as part of Garland Publishing's "Fifty Classics of Crime Fiction" project, under the editorship of Jacques Barzun and Wendell Taylor. While there are comments in Upfield's works which would strike us today as condescending, his treatment of Boney and Australian Aboriginal culture not only displays extensive knowledge, but also sympathetic understanding. He is particularly good at showing Boney's plight as he is caught between two cultures and has to combat both societal pressures and his own uncertainties.

Works Cited

Alexie, Sherman. *Indian Killer*. New York: Atlantic Monthly Press, 1996.

Bowen, Peter. *Coyote Wind*. New York: St. Martin's Press, 1994.

Bowen, Peter. *Notches*. New York: St. Martin's Press, 1997.

Bowen, Peter. *Specimen Song*. New York: St. Martin's Press, 1995.

Bowen, Peter. *Wolf, No Wolf*. New York: St. Martin's Press, 1996.

Carr, A. A. *Eye Killers*. American Indian Literature and Critical Studies Series 13. Norman: U of Oklahoma P, 1995.

Cather, Willa S. *The Professor's House*. New York: Knopf, 1925.

Cather, Willa S. *The Song of the Lark*. Boston: Houghton Mifflin, 1915.

Coel, Margaret. *The Dream Stalker*. New York: Berkley Prime Crime, 1997.

Coel, Margaret. *The Eagle Catcher*. Boulder: U of Colorado P, 1995.

Coel, Margaret. *The Ghost Walker*. New York: Berkley Prime Crime, 1996.

Doss, James D. *The Shaman Laughs*. New York: St. Martin's Press, 1995.

Doss, James D. *The Shaman Sings*. New York: St. Martin's Press, 1994.

Doss, James D. *The Shaman's Bones*. New York: Avon Books, 1997.

Freese, Peter. "Joe Leaphorn as Cultural Mediator in Tony Hillerman's Mysteries." *American Popular Culture at Home and Abroad*. Ed. Lewis H. Carlson and Kevin B. Vichcales. Kalamazoo: New Issues Press, 1996. 101–32.

Gray, Muriel. *The Trickster*. New York: Doubleday, 1995.

Hager, Jean. *The Fire Carrier*. New York: The Mysterious Press (Warner Books), 1995.

Hager, Jean. *Ghostland*. New York: The Mysterious Press (Warner Books), 1992.

Hager, Jean. *The Grandfather Medicine*. New York: St Martin's Press, 1989.

Hager, Jean. *Nightwalker*. New York: St. Martin's Press, 1990.

Hager, Jean. *Ravenmocker*. New York: The Mysterious Press (Warner Books), 1992.

Hager, Jean. *The Redbird's Cry*. New York: The Mysterious Press (Warner Books), 1995.

Hager, Jean. *Seven Black Stones*. New York: The Mysterious Press (Warner Books), 1996.

Hager, Jean. *Spirit Catcher*. New York: The Mysterious Press (Warner Books), 1997.

Hillerman, Tony. *Blessing Way*. New York: Harper and Row, 1970.

Hillerman, Tony. *Coyote Waits*. New York: Harper and Row, 1990.

Hillerman, Tony. *Dance Hall of the Dead*. New York: Harper and Row, 1973.

Hillerman, Tony. *The Dark Wind.* New York: Harper and Row, 1982.

Hillerman, Tony. *The Fallen Man.* New York: Harper Collins, 1996.

Hillerman, Tony. *Ghostway.* New York: Harper and Row, 1984.

Hillerman, Tony. *Listening Woman.* New York: Harper and Row, 1978.

Hillerman, Tony. *People of Darkness.* New York: Harper and Row, 1980.

Hillerman, Tony. *Sacred Clowns.* New York: Harper Collins, 1993.

Hillerman, Tony. *Skinwalkers.* New York: Harper and Row, 1986.

Hillerman, Tony. *Talking God.* New York: Harper and Row, 1989.

Hillerman, Tony. *A Thief of Time.* New York: Harper and Row, 1988.

Holt, Patricia. "Tony Hillerman." *Publishers Weekly* 24 October 1980: 6.

Lackey, Mercedes. *Sacred Ground.* New York: Tom Doherty Associates (TOR Books), 1994.

Medawar, Mardi Oakley. *Death at Rainy Mountain.* New York: St. Martin's Press, 1996.

Medawar, Mardi Oakley. *Witch of the Palo Duro.* New York: St. Martin's Press, 1997.

Owens, Louis. *Bone Game.* American Indian Literature and Critical Studies Series 10. Norman: U of Oklahoma P, 1994.

Owens, Louis. *Nightland.* New York: Dutton, 1996.

Owens, Louis. *The Sharpest Sight.* American Indian Literature and Critical Studies Series 1. Norman: U of Oklahoma P, 1992.

Paretsky, Sara. *Tunnel Vision*. New York: Delacorte, 1994.

Penn, W. S. *All My Sins Are Relatives*. Lincoln: U of Nebraska P, 1995.

Perry, Thomas. *Dance for the Dead*. New York: Random House, 1996.

Perry, Thomas. *Shadow Woman*. New York: Random House, 1997.

Perry, Thomas. *Vanishing Act*. New York: Random House, 1995.

Reynolds, Brad. *A Ritual Death*. New York: Avon Books, 1997.

Reynolds, Brad. *The Story Knife*. New York: Avon Books, 1996.

Sahlins, Marshall. *Culture and Practical Reason*. Chicago: U of Chicago P, 1976.

Salisbury, Neal. "American Indians and American History." *The American Indian and the Problem of History*. Ed. Calvin Martin. New York: Oxford UP, 1987. 46–54.

Sanders, William. *Blood Autumn*. New York: St. Martin's Press, 1996.

Silko, Leslie Marmon. *Almanac of the Dead*. New York: Simon and Schuster, 1991.

Smith, Martin Cruz. *Gorky Park*. New York: Random House, 1981.

Smith, Martin Cruz. *Nightwing*. New York: W. W. Norton, 1977.

Smith, Martin Cruz. *Rose*. New York: Random House, 1996

Smith, Martin Cruz. *Stallion Gate*. New York: Random House, 1986.

Stabenow, Dana. *Blood Will Tell*. New York: Putnam, 1996.

Stabenow, Dana. *Breakup*. New York: Putnam, 1997.

Stabenow, Dana. *A Cold-Blooded Business*. New York: Berkley Books, 1994.

Stabenow, Dana. *A Cold Day for a Murder*. New York: Berkley Books, 1992.

Stabenow, Dana. *Dead in the Water*. New York: Berkley Books, 1993.

Stabenow, Dana. *A Fatal Thaw*. New York: Berkley Books, 1992.

Stabenow, Dana. *Play with Fire*. New York: Berkley Books, 1995.

Thurlo, David, and Aimée Thurlo. *Bad Medicine*. New York: Forge, 1997.

Thurlo, David, and Aimée Thurlo. *Blackening Song*. New York: Forge, 1995.

Thurlo, David, and Aimée Thurlo. *Death Walker*. New York: Forge, 1996.

Upfield, Arthur William. *The Bone Is Pointed*. Garden City, NY: Doubleday, 1947.

Young, Scott. *Murder in a Cold Climate*. New York: Viking, 1989.

Young, Scott. *The Shaman's Knife*. New York: Viking, 1993.

Zolbrod, Paul. *Reading the Voice: Native American Poetry on the Page*. Salt Lake City: U of Utah P, 1995.

11

King and Kodachrome:
Green Grass, Running Water's
Models for Non-Native Participation

Maurice Collins

In *Medicine River,* Will Horse Capture never responds to the white woman he meets at the cocktail party who is surprised to learn that he is a photographer. She asks, "'Kind of ironic isn't it?...the way Indians feel about photographs'" (*Medicine River* 229). In a 1990 interview, King explains that Will does not need to answer because "the question itself is enough to remind the reader of the range of stereotypes and clichés" (Rooke 62). However, King's explanation isn't really an explanation—keeping him consistent with the ethos he has constructed in both *Medicine River* and *Green Grass, Running Water.*

His discussion of photography elsewhere in *Medicine River* suggests that it and its implications are more complicated than his explicit interview statements make it seem. His treatment of photography in *Green Grass, Running Water,* and especially of its relationship to the sacred, further implies this complexity. By offering a range of responses to the sacred, King models appropriate and inappropriate non-Native responses and cultivates a readership that is more comfortable with the silences surrounding the sacred and therefore more likely to respond properly. Clearly, however, it doesn't always work.

Percy Walton contends that "In *Medicine River*, a positive Native presence is generated through its difference from the negative attributes that the Native has been made to signify within the English-Canadian discourse" (Walton 79). He further asserts that King does this "by constructing a presence upon the absence of the native Other." However, in his essay "Godzilla vs. Postcolonial," King suggests that he sees what he has done as something quite different. While King does not address Walton directly, he argues, "The full complement of terms—precolonial, colonial, and postcolonial—reek of unabashed ethnocentrism and well-meaning dismissal...[the concept] assumes that the starting point for that discussion is the advent of Europeans in North America...it also assumes that the struggle between guardian and ward is the catalyst for contemporary Native literature" ("Godzilla" 11–12). In his introduction to *All My Relations*, King maintains the necessity of creating, "a particular kind of world in which the Judeo-Christian concern with good and evil and order and disorder is *replaced* with the more native concern for balance and harmony" (xiii, emphasis mine). Walton has committed the very error with which King charges the well-intentioned-but-ultimately-mistaken. King has not, as Walton claims, constructed upon the silences left by preceding Euro-Canadians. Nor has he written in opposition to a preconceived Other. King has developed literature that is self-sufficient, replete with silences of its own, and possessed of the elements necessary to create a non-Native audience capable of understanding and appreciating it on its own terms.

Photography

The most obvious and readily understandable entry into King's method is through his discussion of photography. In *Green Grass, Running Water* nearly all the discussion of photography centers around the ban on it at the Sun Dance. Will Horse Capture's work is mentioned in *Green Grass* but only insofar as he makes the fake photos for Latisha's Dead Dog Cafe. In *Medicine River*, however, the discussion of Will's work and photography in general is far more extensive and implies, even states, that some forms of photography are positive and desirable while others are to be avoided. Will's primary occupation is that of a portraitist—in this form of photography the subjects willingly engage, and they retain a great deal of control over it. The enthusiasm with which Harlen encourages Will to set up shop in *Medicine River* sharply contrasts the simplicity of the statement made by the woman at the cocktail party. Harlen states unequivocally that "Pictures of the family are good things to have" (*Medicine River* 215) and Lionel, a respected elder and storyteller from the reserve, offers similar approval (*Medicine River* 169).

Perhaps most telling is Harlen's argument that Will ought to set up shop in *Medicine River* because it is "'Real embarrassing for us to have to go to a white for something intimate like a picture'" (*Medicine River* 94). He also wants a picture of himself and Will standing over Custer's grave at Little Big Horn Memorial so he can send it to their community newspaper. Harlen has even scripted the caption that would run under it. In these instances, Harlen has hit upon two crucial elements in the distinction between appropriate and inappropriate uses of photography—a respect for intimacy and the subjects' control over the presentation of their own selves.

King tells Rooke, "'I'm questioning the position of the person who's making the choices...the important thing for me is that the artist is a part of that community'" (63). At the outset of the novel, Harlen attempts to get Will tribal funds to start his business but is reminded that there are no loans for non-status Indians—clearly establishing Will as an outsider. Even so, Will creates and maintains a link to the community of the reserve and does service to that community through his photography for the Friendship Centre. When Bertha comes to talk him into doing this work for free—as she does repeatedly—she maintains, "'You got responsibilities, you know'" (*Medicine River* 177). King identifies Will's inclusion, at the invitation of the others, in the group photo as the moment at which Will moves closer to becoming a real part of that community (Rooke 63).

The questions raised by these instances are featured in Will's most elaborate fantasy in which his journalist father's "superb piece on traditional and contemporary Maori life" is scrapped when the elders decide that they "would prefer that he didn't put their pictures in a magazine" (*Medicine River* 85). The request for privacy and control by the Maoris results immediately in Will's father placing his "superb story ...and all the film" on the fire. Again, photography is at issue not in and of itself but because of the uses to which it might be put and because of the effect it has on self-representation. Less clear is Will's real-life stance on the issue. He is asked to use his own judgment in photographing an exhibition of an artist's war shirts (*Medicine River* 105). We are never told what Will's judgment is.

The inclusion of Will Horse Capture as a tangential member of the community of *Green Grass, Running Water* is an invitation to import to *Green Grass* the concerns presented in *Medicine River*. In *Green Grass*, King offers two examples of white men attempting to photograph the Sun Dance. The tourist from Michigan stumbles upon it and doesn't know he's doing wrong at first, but he refuses to cooperate when Eli's uncle asks, firmly but politely, for the film. King makes clear that the issue is not one of secrecy because, as Eli remembers, occasionally tourists—sometimes invited, other times by chance—would come to camp without anyone being hostile (*Green Grass* 151).

George Morningstar, however, perpetrates his illicit photography deliberately, knowing full well that it is not allowed. Latisha admonishes him, but, consistent with the earlier incident, she still does not require him to leave. George is the poster boy for how *not* to participate in the sacred, but not simply because he is taking photographs. He responds to Latisha by arguing, "'It's not exactly sacred, is it? More like a campout or a picnic'" (*Green Grass* 20). His argument is accompanied by an understated menace, in that he does not let her move freely. As it becomes clear from the confrontation with Lionel and Eli that he will not get his way, George becomes "florid" and insulting. His arms begin "quivering," recalling the violent abuse he had habitually committed on Latisha and forging a link between it and his attempt to photograph the Sun Dance (*Green Grass* 427). George's claim, at this point in the narrative, to ownership of the ancestral jacket that was suffocating Lionel forges a similarly direct link between the photography, General George Custer's behavior, and John Wayne's films.

This scene also creates a link to George's earlier Sun Dance experience. In his behavior there we can see the seeds that later ripen into violence and sacrilege. He fires questions rapidly at everyone within range, on every conceivable topic from why the dancers skip to what goes on in the double teepee. Latisha's father notes George's propensity for questions and in turn asks Latisha satirical questions about him to express his displeasure (*Green Grass* 367). Latisha's father's complaint seems less with George's curiosity than with how he goes about satisfying it.

Silences

Silence, like photography, receives complicated treatment throughout both novels and it is through his practice of carefully constructed silences that King attempts the balance he tells Rooke he attempted in *Medicine River*, the balance between telling his story and assuring the Native community he is not telling too much. In some ways, however, the questions over what should be silent and how to deal with those silences are more slippery than those surrounding photography. On the one hand, we are told that "'Discretion was not one of Harlen's many admirable characteristics'" and that he "'was more concerned with the free flow of information than with something as greedy as personal privacy'" (*Medicine River* 149). Will says, "'Bertha over at the Friendship Centre called it meddling. Harlen would have thought of it as general maintenance'" (*Medicine River* 31).

Bertha is not the only person on the reserve who sides with discretion. Granny Pete never forgives George for introducing Will's parents, "Just got to show off his relations to whites. No more sense than a horseshoe" (*Medicine River* 8). Will's mother scolds him early in the novel that the letters his father wrote to her are private; she seldom if ever discusses his father and, Will tells us, never uses his father's name (*Medicine River* 128). If Will knows it, he never uses it either. We don't even know Will's last name until more than halfway through the novel and it is his mother's Indian surname—not his father's.

Even Harlen seems to have his limits. When Will asks him about his relationship with his brother, Harlen carefully evades Will's questions before chastising Will for being "so curious about other people's business" (*Medicine River* 155). Will's questioning here seems to be an attempt to locate Harlen's limit—the existence of which Will has only just realized. However, just as Will never mentions his own surname and never tells us his decision about photographing the War Shirts, he never says explicitly how he feels about Harlen.

The Sacred

As in many aspects of Native life and religion, there is no dogma to assist the non-Native reader in understanding the line between propriety and impropriety. Vine Deloria Jr. contends that Native religion is experiential and learned over time from membership in a community. King hopes that one day the "sheer bulk" of Native literature, "when it reaches some sort of critical mass, will present us with a matrix from which a variety of patterns can be discerned" (*Relations* x). Similarly, King instructs non-Natives not with diatribe and lecture but through the sheer bulk and critical mass of reactions to the sacred and to the other silences offered throughout the novel.

The Indian characters, for the most part, show a comfortability with the unexplained the non-Native characters can only approximate. It is not until well after he was spotted that he has the following realizations: "The first was that he was standing ankle-deep in a pool of water. The second was that one of the Indians was wearing a black mask" (*Green Grass* 104). While Lionel finds both of these things curious, he does not seem compelled to seek an explanation but rather content to wait for one to reveal itself.

At the university, Alberta is directly engaged in attempting to teach dull white students about Native culture. She states that one slide in her show of drawings by Native captives "'shouldn't need any explanation'" (*Green Grass* 16). She responds to her student's lame attempt at an explanation with only "a wonderful, rich silence" (*Green Grass* 17). Neither Alberta nor the narrator provides the reader with a description of the drawing in question.

Coyote is particularly problematic at the outset of the First Woman story because, while I do not believe that, as Walton has argued, that Coyote is representative of white people, his behavior in this particular instance is a great deal like George's curiosity. The storyteller, instructing Coyote in appropriate behaviors, seems unwilling to offer a detailed explanation for Ahdamn's presence in First Woman's garden. When Coyote continues to show his curiosity towards the end of First Woman's story, the storyteller instructs Coyote to be patient, to wait for the patterns to reveal themselves, and to accept those things that cannot be explained. Coyote's behavior here, when viewed in relation to his later actions is based more on disingenuity than a lack of understanding. Not all the Indian characters in the novel behave consistently well in the face of the sacred, but they all know it when they see it, and all find a way to participate in it. Even the most admirable of the non-Native characters fail on this latter count.

Non-Native "Participation"

Dr. Hovaugh has spent much of his career tracking the careers of the four old Indians and recognizes, on some level, that they are connected to power, but, he too just doesn't get it. He adopts a guardian posture toward the four old Indians—the very posture of which King is so critical. When lecturing Babo on the difference between omen and miracle, Hovaugh launches into long-winded, misguided, and ultimately meaningless academic explanation (*Green Grass* 80). His colleague John Eliot shrugs off the disappearance of the Indians as yet another mystery, but Hovaugh was envious of his easy going demeanor (*Green Grass* 50).

Clifford Sifton, despite his involvement in the harmful activity of the dam, shows some promise, identifying at least that Eli has adopted a Bartleby the Scrivener-like approach to the dam. Even so, he shows no awareness of the type of interpretation Lucy Maddox offers for Melville's story. Sifton buys into the same ideology that prevents Bartleby's employer from understanding Bartleby's silence, telling Eli that Bartleby "didn't want to do anything to improve his life" (*Green Grass* 155). Also like Bartleby's employer, Sifton continues to yearn for an explicit and immediate explanation (*Green Grass* 149).

The girl in Latisha's high school class comes closer. The narrator says, "Ann Hubert...asked her if the Sun Dance was like going to church. Latisha tried to think of ways to explain exactly what the Sun Dance was, how the people felt about it, why it was important... . Finally Ann said that it was probably a mystery...like God and Jesus and the Holy Cross. Latisha wanted to tell Ann that it wasn't, but in the end she said nothing" (*Green Grass* 408). From this it seems that an acceptance of mystery does not entail giving up all attempts to understand. The Sun Dance can be understood, just not by Ann Hubert—at least not in the way she wants.

Of all the white characters, there seems to be the most hope for Karen. She seems to make honest efforts both to understand Eli and his culture and to respect their desires to be left alone. When invited to the Sun Dance by Norma, Karen is flattered, recognizing the intimate personal nature of the Sun Dance and, when told she can't photograph, readily grasps at least a part of the desire for self-representation. Upon their return to Toronto, Karen defers to Eli on questions from friends about the Sun Dance, displaying a heightened sense of care. When she does so, Eli realizes that he does not have the answers to all the questions (*Green Grass* 316). It is not that Eli does not want to explain; rather, like Latisha, he just can not.

Somehow, Karen has missed the point. She remembers, "'All those tepees,'" but Eli remembers "'the people'" (*Green Grass* 287). Similarly, she cannot grasp and he cannot explain his reasons for not going back and it becomes "a silent place in their relationship" (*Green Grass* 316).

The non-Native character who comes closest to appropriate behavior in the face of the sacred is Babo Jones who is black and a woman and the only one who knows the four old Indians are women. Cereno, Hovaugh, and the others, however, choose to believe the authority of "the files" over the authority of direct oral testimony and so believe the Indians to be men. Unlike Hovaugh, who argues the gender of the Indians, Babo responds by simply saying "'Suit yourself.'"

Like her eponymous grandfather—the Babo of Melville's *Benito Cereno*—Babo Jones refuses to correct the misconceptions and shortsightedness of the white people around her and bamboozles the impressionable Delano with a story. Not unlike the power the four old Indians exercise over the technology of the film, Babo's telling of the story causes the tape recorder to distort its mechanism. Perhaps most importantly, Babo makes clear that it is the Indians' story and that she is "'just repeating it as a favor.'"

Like First Woman, Babo enjoys a good adventure. Like Lionel and Alberta's mother, she is nonplused by the water surrounding her blue pinto and seems equally unsurprised and unupset when the car goes missing. She repeats "'isn't that the trick,'" when Hovaugh's car also goes missing, when the four old Indians remake the Western and again when she and Hovaugh view the omen/miracle, that neither she nor the narrator makes any attempt to describe or explain to the reader. In additon, despite Hovaugh's agitation at seeing the cars and witnessing the breaking of the dam, she says only "'Isn't that the trick'" (447).

Babo's behavior would seem exemplary, but she is still a non-participant, watching the events from the seat of a bus, through a window. The appearances of the sacred in the novel ultimately serve to reconnect the members of the Indian community. While Babo finds these appearances interesting, they do not serve to connect her in the same way.

Despair?

About the literature he calls "associational," King maintains that, even though non-Native readers may become, in a sense, associated with Native communities by reading the literature, they will not be able to become truly a part of them ("Godzilla"14; Rooke 74). For the white audience in particular, he holds out less hope than for the more general category of non-Native: "'I really don't care about the white audience. They don't have an understanding of the intricacies of native life, and I don't think they're much interested in it quite frankly'" (Weaver 57).

King's concerns are certainly borne out by James McManus' *New York Times* review of *Green Grass, Running Water*. McManus complains at the "proliferation" of "unlikely convergences and apocalyptic reversals" and at "the cast of human and mythological characters Mr. King has brought into play [which] has become large, confusing and exceedingly talkative," a "prolixity [which] causes the novel to lose momentum" (McManus 21). Clearly, McManus is not sufficiently interested in those intricacies to wait for the pattern (the same type of pattern King discussed in "Godzilla vs. Postcolonial") to emerge from the critical mass of the novel itself. In his paper, "Mother Tongues and Native Voices," Scott Stevens talks about linguistic despair—the idea that Native and Anglo cultures will never find a common language, and it seems that some similar form of despair is precisely what King has fallen into, and it seems that reviews like this one have given him good cause.

Even if King is right that non-Natives are ultimately outsiders, he seems also to believe, maybe only to hope, that we can still learn to better recognize the sacred and to behave more appropriately in its presence. This should be our hope as well. We can come to that recognition only from thoughtful observation, the patience to wait for the sacred to reveal itself, and the acceptance that it might not. Without these, we critics will continue to behave as if we have no relations.

Works Cited

Deloria, Vine, Jr. *God Is Red*. Golden, CO: Fulcrum, 1994.

King, Thomas. *Green Grass, Running Water*. New York: Bantam, 1993.

King, Thomas. "Godzilla vs. Postcolonial." *World Literature Written in English* 30.2 (1990): 10–16.

King, Thomas. "Introduction." *All My Relations: An Anthology of Canadian Native Fiction*. Norman: U of Oklahoma P, 1992. ix–xvi.

King, Thomas. *Medicine River*. Toronto: Penguin, 1991.

Maddox, Lucy. *Removals: Nineteenth Century American Literature and the Politics of Indian Affairs*. New York: Oxford U P, 1991.

McManus, James. "Has Red Dog Gone White?" Rev. of *Green Grass, Running Water* by Thomas King. *New York Times Book Review* 25 July 1993: 7, 21.

Melville, Herman. *Bartleby* and *Benito Cereno*. New York: Dover, 1991.

Rooke, Constance. "Interview with Tom King." *World Literature Written in English* 30.2 (1990): 62–76.

Stevens, Scott. "Mother Tongues and Native Voices." *American Indian Literatures and Cultures*. PCA/ACA Conference. 27 March 1997.

Walton, Percy. "'Tell Our Own Stories': Politics and the Fiction of Thomas King." *World Literature Written in English* 30.2 (1990): 77–84.

Weaver, Jace. "PW Interviews: Thomas King." *Publishers Weekly* 8 March 1993: 56–57.

12

Dialectic to Dialogic: Negotiating Bicultural Heritage in Sherman Alexie's Sonnets

Carrie Etter

As James Clifford notes in *The Predicament of Culture,* cultural contact has consistently been portrayed as either "absorption by the other *or* resistance to the other," a dichotomizing event (344). However, is it ever so absolute? What do we make of Sherman Alexie's sonnets? Because they lack rhyme and meter, hence avoiding the strictures of Western form, do we interpret them as acts of resistance? Or does Alexie's willingness to undertake Western forms, among them the sonnet and the villanelle, suggest his absorption? Clifford goes on to ask, "…what identity is conceived not as a boundary to be maintained but as a nexus of relations and transactions actively engaging a subject?" (344). Through his sonnets, Alexie negotiates between his cultural inheritances, Coeur d'Alene/Spokane and Anglo American, a negotiation that enables the speaker of his poems to move from the stance of a passive observer to an active participant. Simultaneously, Alexie's restructuring of the sonnet enables him to upset the reader's expectation of resolution and thus promote the idea that the Indian dilemma is never a matter that can be easily or hastily solved.

From his first book, *The Business of Fancydancing*, Alexie modifies the English sonnet to handle its traditional themes—death and romantic love—as well as a different concern, familial relations. These sonnets utilize the traditional grouping of elements of a problem, and yet rather than employ the English three quatrains and a couplet, Alexie uses three tercets and one quatrain, making each thirteen lines. In *The Business of Fancydancing* and *Old Shirts & New Skins*, Alexie rejects the couplet, and more importantly, its function of resolving the preceding progression. Barbara Herrnstein Smith, in *Poetic Closure: A Study of How Poems End,* notes the widely held belief that the terminal couplet of the English sonnet makes for "striking resolution," yet qualifies this by saying it derives its force from the formal structure that precedes it. Even so, I argue that the English sonnet's presentation and development of an apparent dilemma also lead to an expectation of resolution. Thus, each of the sonnets works against resolution, urging that every Indian dilemma resists the pat denouement of the English sonnet.

Even so, the agency such action seems to offer eludes the speaker within the poems themselves. In "Indian Boy Love Song (#4)," the speaker reflects on his father's alcoholism and at the end waits at his window, "dreaming / bottles / familiar in [his] hands, not [his] father's, always / empty." "Sudden Death" ends similarly; the speaker describes his father's memory of a football game in which he missed the field goal and his father's consequent desire to relive and revise that moment. Watching football on TV over twenty years later, his father,

> roaring past the fourth quarter like a train
>
> leaving a lover behind, stands eagle-armed
> on the platform, whistling for God and 1956
> to pick him up, carry him on their shoulders.

All of the speakers in *The Business of Fancydancing*'s eight sonnets present observers who only watch and record, ending in ambivalence and yearning for change.

This passivity results from a dialectic positioning. In these sonnets, Alexie divides his world into an American Indian us and an Anglo American them. The pervasiveness of this division evinces itself most vividly in "Indian Boy Love Song (#3)."

> I remember when I told
> my cousin
> she was more beautiful
>
> than any white girl
> I had ever seen.
> She kissed me then
> with both lips, a tongue
>
> that tasted clean and un-

clean at the same time
like the river which divides

the heart of my heart, all
the beautiful white girls on one side,
my beautiful cousin on the other.

By naming the river with both its Indian and its Anglo sides "the heart of
[his] heart," Alexie acknowledges his bicultural inheritance, and both the
white girls and the cousin appear similarly beautiful at the end as opposed
to the distinguishing compliment he gives his cousin earlier in the poem.
He feels compelled to align himself with the American Indian side despite
his realization of a bicultural identity. Similarly, in "November 22, 1983,"
the father "for twenty years [whispers]" to his wife "'ain't no Indian loves
Marilyn Monroe.'" The title of the poem dates the twentieth anniversary
of former president John F. Kennedy's death, suggesting that since
Kennedy's death the father has claimed and reclaimed an identity opposed
to the Anglo American Kennedy who presumably "loves Marilyn Monroe."
Apparently the son learns from his father's model of an identity defined,
in part, by difference. This reluctance to claim a bicultural identity arises,
in part, from the speaker's self-identification as other; as Leslie Ullman
recognizes in her review of *The Business of Fancydancing,* Alexie's
characters "are free to leave and often do, only to find themselves facing
another kind of boundary, a sense of being foreigners, bound more than
they realized by a sense of where they came from and who they are" (187).
As American Indians in an Anglo culture, Alexie's characters cling to their
Indianness, at least partially, by announcing their differences from whites;
any acknowledgment of an Anglo inheritance is not voiced aloud.

Yet claiming, even embracing, one's American Indian identity is not
enabling in Alexie's 13-line sonnet. That identity comes with a historicity
of inability to determine one's own fate, as it is limited again and again by
the changing regulations and policies of the U.S. government. How does
one claim that historically bound identity and yet forge the empowerment
of agency that has been so long curtailed or denied? Ullman continues,
"Many characters in this book are shown in a no-win situation at the end
of a scene or poem, simply waiting 'for something to change' or to
'happen,' like the group of Indian boys on their way home from a

basketball tournament, out of food, their car out of gas in the middle of the night on a cold highway in 'Traveling'" (15). Other characters are caught in a kind of no-man's-land between dreams that will never be realized and memories of past glory..." (187). Alexie's speaker aligns himself with his American Indian identity and finds himself locked into its historical lack of agency, despite the sonnets' irresolution and consequent insistence on an alternate vision.

In part, the lack of agency results from Alexie's insistence on a dialectic. David L. Moore explains, "A dialogic...makes visible the possibility of exchange without dominance or co-optation, whereas the dialectic is haunted by the hierarchies of dominance inherent in dualism" (18). To claim Indianness in and of itself is to reinforce the traditional Anglo-Indian hierarchy, and that reinforcement ultimately disables the speaker, rendering him a passive recorder. This is the one ability that remains: to record the experience without romanticization. As Jennifer Gillian notes, "Rejecting both nostalgia for Indian life as it was and a claim for his own authenticity as one who knows Indian experience, Alexie struggles against the tendency to romanticize the past that he sees in much Native American writing" (95–96); Alexie's use of the sonnet enables him to render American Indian experience with greater authenticity by denying resolution, even as his insistence on a dialectic disempowers the speaker's agency.

Even though agency eludes the speaker, it does not elude Alexie. While any reader might identify the sonnets' inherent irresolution, a reader trained in Western poetics would be more likely to follow the sonnet progression and expect the resolution Alexie denies. In *The Mirror and the Killer-Queen: Otherness in Literary Language,* Gabriele Schwab supports Wolfgang Iser's claim that "texts carry within themselves their own model according to which they attempt to shape their contact with readers." That is, the text possesses "strategies of communication, its 'guiding devices' that exert a certain control by inviting or privileging specific responses." These devices give rise to a "textual agency that actively confirms, interferes with, or disrupts a culture's familiar communicative patterns that are presumably internalized by its readers" (19). Alexie's sonnets enact their irresolution most effectively with the reader most informed in Western/Anglo poetics, disrupting her expectations for resolution. The

Anglo-Indian hierarchical dialectic remains, and yet Alexie finds a way, within that hierarchy, to communicate, even as his poems' speakers remain disabled by the focus on a dialectic split between cultures.

This dialectic becomes more entrenched in Alexie's next book, *Old Shirts & New Skins*, as the sonnets focus on American Indian identity and become much more ironic in tone. Discussing Franz Boas's *Race, Language, Culture* in *Ethnocriticism*, Arnold Krupat remarks, "[W]hat is true of irony thematically, as an 'attitude,' is true of irony structurally, as a form, as well: ironic structures achieve their effects by frustrating conventional expectations for climax and closure" (94). Alexie has created an ironic structure in his sonnet, "frustrating conventional expectations for...closure"; he insists to an implied readership which includes American Indians and Anglo Americans that any Indian dilemma cannot be hastily resolved. In "Architecture," the speaker becomes speakers; the individual American Indian becomes all reservation Indians in an inclusive "we" which implies a "they" who created this confining and defining "architecture" of the reservation. "Translated from the American" makes the dialectic relationship between whites and Indians both explicit and divisive. "[A]fter all the drive-in theaters have closed," the speaker plans to "make camp alone" and "replay westerns," "wait[ing] for white boys / climbing fences to watch this Indian speak." While plural fences separate the races, suggesting a greater divide between them than race alone, the whites can climb over these fences to enter Indian territory—or so they think. One fence is race, another is language—one that, as the end of the poem indicates, the whites cannot surmount.

Nevertheless, despite this racial and cultural division, the imagined space becomes the place for action. The speaker concludes not with reflection but with a response: "...when they ask 'how' / I'll give them exact directions." This gives rise to the two visionary sonnets of *First Indian on the Moon*. There, the form changes from the 13-line structure to a structure more closely paralleling the English sonnet form with three quatrains and an ostensible couplet at the end. Yet these couplets do not resolve the preceding dilemma. Even within a closer approximation to the Western form, Alexie retains the irresolution; these couplets reflect on the preceding dilemma summarily without resolving it—if anything, they work to lodge the irresolution more firmly.

These poems come to terms with a dual cultural inheritance by deriving their visions from a cultural dialogic. Even so, this does not diminish Alexie's or his speaker's claim to an American Indian identity. As Moore asserts, "...[D]ialogical survival...maintains difference within the dynamics of opposition" and "[n]on-oppositional dialogics does not mean 'harmony' or 'communication,' any more than it means conciliation or complicity" (17). In "I Would Steal Horses," the speaker imagines all that he would do for his lover and hence for himself; the lack of what he has to give results as much from his own weaknesses as from historical ramifications. The speaker finds the basis of his identity not in a divisive "us/them," but in an inclusive we—an enabling American Indian identity without a dialectic opposition. While the activity is imaginary, it does release the paralysis of the historical, hierarchical dialectic that persisted in the 13-line sonnets.

"The Game Between the Jews and the Indians Is Tied Going into the Bottom of the Ninth Inning" demonstrates this cultural dialogic most effectively. Alexie recognizes a similarity between the Jews and Indians—a history of suffering and injustice intertwined with a history of survival. The cultural contact is not between two hierarchically divided groups but between two groups engaged in a similar struggle for cultural survival. The very act of this imagined game—tied at the bottom of the ninth—goes beyond the memories of suffering to create a reminder of their joint survival, offering action (the reminding) in place of passive observation.

> So, now, when you touch me
> my skin, will you think
> of Sand Creek, Wounded Knee?
> And what will I remember
>
> when your skin is next to mine
> Auschwitz, Buchenwald?
> No, we will only think of the past
> as one second before
>
> where we are now, the future
> just one second ahead
> but every once in a while
> we can remind each other

that we are both survivors and children
and grandchildren of survivors.

As Schwab says, "As a medium of cultural contact, the experimental forms of poetic language are instruments in an aesthetic experience that may well form a countersocialization—as long as literature retains its subversive potential" (46). Through his sonnets, Alexie "countersocializes" his reader to accept the irresolution inherent in American Indian experience, revising the Western belief that action solves. What imagination and irresolution together create is the potential for agency—not as a move toward a definitive solution but, through the imagined dialogic, a place where the hierarchical dialectic cannot impose its historically bound limitations, and thus, a place that enables agency for the native speaker.

Works Cited

Alexie, Sherman. *The Business of Fancydancing: Stories and Poems.*
Brooklyn, NY: Hanging Loose P, 1992.

Alexie, Sherman. *First Indian on the Moon.* Brooklyn, NY: Hanging
Loose P, 1993.

Alexie, Sherman. *Old Shirts & New Skins.* Los Angeles: American Indian
Studies Center, UCLA, 1993.

Clifford, James. *The Predicament of Culture: Twentieth Century
Ethnography, Literature, and Art.* Cambridge, MA: Harvard U P,
1988.

Gillian, Jennifer. "Reservation Home Movies: Sherman Alexie's Poetry."
American Literature 68.1 (1996): 91–110.

Krupat, Arnold. *Ethnocriticism: Ethnography, History, Literature.*
Berkeley: U of California P, 1992.

Moore, David L. "Decolonizing Criticism: Reading Dialectics and
Dialogics in Native American Literatures." *Studies in American Indian
Literatures* 6.4 (1994): 7–33.

Schwab, Gabriele. *The Mirror and the Killer-Queen: Otherness in Literary
Language.* Bloomington: Indiana UP, 1996.

Smith, Barbara Herrnstein. *Poetic Closure: A Study of How Poems End.*
Chicago: U of Chicago P, 1968.

Ullman, Leslie.   "Review of *The Business of Fancydancing.*" *Kenyon Review* 15.3 (1993): 182–97.

13

Tales of Burning Love:
Louise Erdrich's "Scarlet Letter"

Tom Matchie

Amy Tan, in an address on National Public Radio, said she would rather be recognized as an American author than classified among multicultural writers as Chinese American. The same might be said of Louise Erdrich, perhaps "the foremost practitioner" of Native American fiction (Max 117). She is most often represented as a mixed-blood, and much of the critical analysis of her fiction centers around her use of Chippewa mythology as a key to illusive meaning in her novels. It is also true, however, that Erdrich is an ardent student of American literary history and culture. One only has to look for references to Melville's *Moby Dick* in *Love Medicine* (1984), Flannery O'Connor's notion of the Christian grotesque permeating *Tracks* (1988), or Lipsha's language and naiveté resembling those of Huckleberry Finn in *The Bingo Palace* (1992). I would like to suggest that her fifth novel, *Tales of Burning Love* (1996), is her contemporary answer to the classic nineteenth-century American romantic novel, *The Scarlet Letter*.

Hester's "Selves" as Model for Five Wives

Those familiar with Hawthorne's plot know that Hester Prynne goes through many stages, manifesting in different contexts various "selves." There is the past self with her husband, Roger Chillingworth, a physician for whom she feels "no love" (51) and leaves behind in Europe. Next, there is her past secret self with the minister, Arthur Dimmesdale, including a sexual act she later claims had "a consecration of its own" (140). Ironically, though some would brand her with a "hot iron" (38) for her "sin," she emerges as a kind of saint, an image of "sinless motherhood" (41). A third tragic self is the Hester who promises Chillingworth she will keep his identity "secret" (58), while he pursues his destructive vengeance on Dimmesdale. Still, another more assertive self surfaces in the forest with her pastor. After confessing her "deception" (139), she throws off the scarlet letter and confronts Arthur directly with the "weight of misery" (142) that this society has laid on him. Her honest talk of love and freedom (their leaving together for Europe) triggers in him a radical change—a "revolution" of "thought and feeling" (155) that borders on the comical. However, Hester's most pervasive self is the practical role she plays in public. In spite of either man or her own "shame," her sewing and other service causes the townspeople to "love her" (Baym 58), and in this context she outlasts the other major characters in the novel. All things considered, there are at least five different postures (selves) that Hester takes toward reality in Hawthorne's Puritan love story.

Tales of Burning Love is a contemporary romance set in "the beautiful bleak landscape" (Childress) in and near Fargo, North Dakota. It depicts not one but five "sharp portraits" (Curwen 39) of women with "fully individualized voices" (Lee 30), all married to but one man, Jack Mauser, a mixed up, mixed-blood, construction engineer. Neither religious like Dimmesdale, nor scientific as is Chillingworth, Jack is Erdrich's rendition of the modern (rather than a Puritan) male—one who has unfortunately buried "the Ojibwa part" of himself (152). However, it is through him, or the relationships of the women to him, that Erdrich explores such Hawthorne-like themes as the mystery of love between the sexes, the inner and outer worlds through which it is manifested, the dubious connection of sexuality to religion, and how various types of personalities enter into and affect a marriage or lovers' union. In fact, if one takes these women separately, they might be seen as Hester's different selves relating to "a man," in this case, Jack, as well as to the public. Less moralistic and more humorous than Hawthorne, in *Tales* Erdrich may have written her "funniest, sexiest, most optimistic" novel (Harris). Even so, she is every bit the romantic as Hawthorne, filling her plot with images of nature, particularly sunshine and snow, but especially fire, to accompany each of the wives' distinctive, "burning" tale of love.

June's "Chilling" Experience

Jack's first wife is June Morrissey. In *Love Medicine* and *The Bingo Palace*, and now in *Tales*, June jumps from a truck near Williston in 1981 to get away from its drunken driver, apparently after meeting him in a bar only hours before. We now know from *Tales* that that man was Jack Mauser, and that he and June were united in a "one-night marriage" (382). The episode is important, not only because June's presence permeates at least three of Erdrich's novels, but because it exemplifies a particular kind of love, one not far removed from that characterizing the marriage of Hester Prynne and Roger Chillingworth. That, too, happened in the past. Never even feigning love, she fled to America to escape the man; in Erdrich's novel, June had jumped from the pickup and walked away to her death. Roger pursues Hester anyway; and in *Tales* we learn later that Jack thinks regretfully of his botched sexual affair with June. Later, having burned down his house and faked his own death, he comes to the rescue of his mourning ex-wives caught in the snowstorm, where each has been telling her tale of love. On the way he imagines June "wearing a wedding dress" and "bringing him home" (385). Though some see Jack as simply "a loser" (Hoffert), Michael Lee says Jack's other marriages represent a long-time effort to "recapture the love" he had for June (30), one (unlike Chillingworth's) that is finally fulfilled in Eleanor.

Eleanor: Sexy or Saintly?

The woman in *Tales* most concerned, even preoccupied, with sex is Eleanor Schlick, Jack's second wife. As with Hester, Eleanor has a curious sexual past, ironically coupled with a "saintly" present. Nobody in the Puritan community shares Hester's private life, for the object of her love remains "a riddle," and of him Hester "refuseth to speak" (45). As time goes on, however, Hester emerges as a virtual saint, in spite of the Puritan authorities and the people's initial scorn. In her "Divine Maternity" (44) she walks among them as the mother of Pearl and sews garments for the rich and poor as a virtual New Testament model. Stubbs says Hawthorne represents her as a "madonna of Renaissance art" that contrasts with the rigid Puritan code (84). Others speak of a "spiritual greatness" that transcends her own weakness, the Puritan society, and Hawthorne himself (Carpenter 179). This is not to say that Hester is a saint, any more than that she and Arthur are able to get together as lovers, for their motives—which Crews says are "inaccessible to the conscious will" (146)—are different. It only suggests that Hester's protecting the identity of her lover—who does not share her transcendental vision—is in itself a sacrifice of self that is the stuff of saints rather than sinners.

In *Tales* Erdrich in turn juxtaposes Eleanor's sexual past with the present in the context of sainthood, though her method is different, often comic. A novelist whose "eye for sensual detail is impeccable" (Rev. of *Tales of Burning Love*, *Publishers Weekly*), she even shares with the reader graphic aspects of Eleanor's former erotic life, including intimate thoughts she remembers from her diary:

> *He turns me on my back carefully and kneels, his thighs just under my hips.... He comes into me, comes again, quietly and emotionally, looking into my eyes. "You're the one," he says...and we keep going, fuck ourselves stupid.* (237)

We also know a great deal more about Eleanor's past than we do about Hester's. Specifically, her mother, Anna, was rejected by her father, Lawrence Schlick, a noted funeral director in Fargo, over a past sexual affair between Anna and Jack Mauser. Strangely enough, Eleanor herself then had an affair with Jack and faked being pregnant as a way of getting her parents back together. She even dressed like a kind of "passive martyr," or "Holy Mary" (239)—a virtual parody of Hawthorne's representation of Hester. After leaving Jack, Eleanor went into teaching, but that didn't allay her "sexual need" (37). Fired for seducing a student, she is now nourishing her spiritual life at a convent in Argus, north of Fargo, while doing research on the first potential mixed-blood saint, Sister Leopolda—whose own story appears in *Tracks* and *Love Medicine*. It is in this context that the spiritual dimension of Eleanor's love life comes into play.

While walking in the convent garden with the saintly nun, whose own prayer is ironically "a tale of burning love" (53), Eleanor has a miraculous experience connected to her past sexual life. Jack, an engineer, catapults over the convent wall in a backhoe bucket at midnight to visit his ex-wife. In a hilarious episode, including "lightning" (58) and thunder, Eleanor and

Sister Leopolda (quite ignorant of what is really happening) end up "worshipping" Jack wrapped in a cloak standing on a pedestal being prepared for a statue of the Virgin Mary. If the whole affair seems like another comic version of something sacred, it also mirrors in a mythic way the union of all great lovers—from the Greek Leda (the name of Jack and Eleanor hoped to give their baby) to Hawthorne's own Hester and Dimmesdale. In each case a dubious sexual union, symbolically if not really, seems to have the blessing of the gods.

After Leopolda expires, Eleanor and Jack meet inside the convent where they continue to discuss their love, often realized in secret, but which they have never been able to make work in marriage, any more than have Hester and Dimmesdale. In Jack and Eleanor's case, though they truly loved each other, "fury burned through" their love (81); "we fought over how we couldn't fight" (251), she says, so she left him—went home to mother, entered college, even flew overseas. In speaking of Hester and Dimmesdale, Hawthorne himself claims that love and hate are often very close (Crews 146); and the same might be said of Eleanor and Jack. Unlike Hawthorne's lovers, however, these two eventually do get together. Late in the novel, after the snowstorm in which she walked away from the Ford Explorer stuck on the airport road in Fargo, Eleanor imagines that the saintly Leopolda appeared and "saved her life" (446)—a life which eventually involves her return to the arms of Jack. Dave Wood notes that the novel, the author's "most sensual," ends with sex on a (religiously symbolic) staircase (E2), testifying once again to the close relationship in Erdrich (as in Hawthorne) of sexuality and religion.

Candace's Tragic Flaw

Jack's third wife is Candace Pantamounty, D.D.S., a dentist, "A professional!" (171). Blonde, beautiful, and "brisk" (Hoffert), she is interested in her own career and dependent on nobody. Free, but self-absorbed, her only companion is her dog, Pepperboy. Candy represents that part of Hester that relates to Roger Chillingworth after he comes to America. Hester, too, is free, for no individual or system—not Roger or the Puritan hierarchy—can touch her being. But then something happens. Chillingworth, who has no "household fire" (53) in his heart, commits

Hester to secrecy about his identity, whereupon he becomes Arthur's "medical advisor" (90), a role he uses to undercut the man he suspects to be Hester's lover. His approach, motivated by revenge, and done with scientific precision, hits at the "heart's entire substance" (102). In this way Chillingworth destroys Dimmesdale's chance at a full human relationship with Hester, and likewise Hester's with Dimmesdale.

In *Tales*, a similar pattern occurs. After a hysterectomy, Candy (a scientific type herself) enjoys frequent sexual episodes with men, for there is no risk of pregnancy. An old classmate of Jack's, she meets him again through a dental appointment, has sex with him, and goes hunting with him along with her dog; then they are married. What kills the marriage is Jack's abuse of Pepperboy. After being bitten, he hits and eventually kills the dog, not realizing what it is doing to Candy. He thinks it is accidental, "a goddamn freak occurrence" (379), but she loses respect for one who misuses "helpless things" (295). Hester's tragic flaw is, in effect that she permits Chillingworth to tantalize her loved one, Dimmesdale, and only realizes it too late. It is that self of Hester's that Candy represents in *Tales*—the part that allows another's abuse of someone or something one loves, and indirectly undercuts a burning love of one's own. Candy is more conscious than Hester of what is going on; in *Tales* it is Jack who doesn't make the connection, but in either case the abuse drives the woman closer to her real lover—in Hester's case Dimmesdale, in Candy's another wife of Jack's, Marlis, who is pregnant with the child Candy would love, but can never have.

Marlis Confronts "Black" Jack

Marlis Cook is Jack's fourth wife. She has no Native blood (like June or Dot—Jack's fifth wife), no intellectual/spiritual bent (like Eleanor), no professional expertise (like Candy). She is simply a blackjack dealer at the B & B Bar—a pastime familiar to Erdrich (Wood E2)—who meets Jack by accident. Quickly she gets "a thing" (315) for him, and becomes pregnant—the only one of the wives to do so. His reaction, however, is to abuse her—"twisted my arm.... Shoved me. Hit me" (329), she says. What distinguishes Marlis, however, is the direct way she responds. She treats Jack like none of the others; she not only tells but shows him what he is like. Marlis is that side of Hester who, when the opportunity comes, speaks directly to Dimmesdale about their relationship. It happens midway in the book when they go into the forest together. Here, in letting down her hair and throwing off the letter A, she shows him what it would take to transcend his Puritan rules, to be free, to share her spirit. Sandeen calls this show of passion the "most moving" part of the book—a time when love itself transcends sin, guilt, shame, hypocrisy (426). In fact, Hawthorne accompanies the event with a "burst of sunshine" (138) in the sky. For Fogel the sun is a natural symbol, "real and indispensable," that is connected with love and never controlled by human law (40).

In Marlis's tale, she meets Jack quite by accident. She is knocked out after touching an electrical cable and Jack revives her. Later, he again "Dutch-rubs" (302) her paralyzed face, giving her new (physical) life. Grateful, she marries him. "I love you so deep," she says, "Love me back" (322–23). But he doesn't. In fact, he doesn't stop manhandling her, psychologically or physically—criticizing her makeup as well as twisting, hitting and shoving her when he learns about the baby. In one way "childlike" (Hoffert), but in another "mature-beyond-her-years" (Childress), Marlis finally concludes: *What the hell do you know about being a woman?*" (327). She is much like Hester, who through her language and gestures gives Dimmesdale a lesson in being a human being, not a product of a religious system.

Marlis's method, however, is unique. She and Jack are in a motel, where she wraps him in duct tape while he is sleeping. When he is powerless, she pierces his ears, plucks his eyebrows, waxes and shaves his legs, and forces him to put on high heels in order to demonstrate what a woman has to go through. Her tactic is a bit different from Hester's with Dimmesdale—external rather than internal—but as with Hester it works, at least temporarily. In the woods Dimmesdale is elated, and dances back to town, a new man, determined to become "wholly the lover and flee from all his obligations to the community" (Sandeen 432). In *Tales* Jack is furious with Marlis, but he gets the point. Later, when Marlis wants to make love, he sees that her action was not a personal vendetta. "I'm using you" (424), she says, and now he responds differently to the "taste" of her hair. Late in the novel, Jack, amid "snow" and "sun" (385), comes to understand and accept many people he had heretofore neglected. He develops a new fire for John Jr., as well as "a piercing love" (387) that looked like his mother, June, Eleanor, "All the women he'd ever loved" (441). Though all this may be the result of a religious experience, much of the credit goes to Marlis. Like Hester, she is a good teacher because she is honest, personal, and direct, though in a modern, violent way that is as shocking as Hawthorne's more subtle psychological approach a century and a half ago.

Efficient, Loyal, Steady Dot

When *Tales of Burning Love* opens, Jack is married to his fifth wife, Dot—the young arrogant girl in *The Beet Queen*, married in *Love Medicine* to Gerry Nanapush, now in (and out) of prison. Like Candace, an old classmate of Jack's from Argus, Dot is still impulsive, marrying Jack on a dare. If Hester's needle makes her a valuable part of the community, Dot's "accounting skills" (14) save Jack's business, making her more a "business associate" (40) than his wife; they even "make love with efficiency" (97). Like Hester, Dot is "loyal" (199) to her mate, and if people love Hester because she makes garments for everybody from Pearl to the Governor, Dot (who also knits) is the most practical among the wives. After Jack's mock funeral—he burns his house as a way of avoiding bankruptcy—Dot insists on seeing and handling Jack's ashes (which don't really exist), pays the funeral bills because she's Jack's latest wife, and drives the others to the B & B Bar in West Fargo to get Marlis's vote on what to do with what's left of Jack. In Hawthorne's novel, Hester is the one character, says Baym, "truly concerned with society and human relations" (407); Dot performs a similar mission in *Tales*. Less passionate than the other wives, she is the self who functions best in public.

Though the community "cannot do without Hester," says Sandeen, she still feels like a "pariah" (427). In Erdrich's novel, Dot is also the loner in the group; June is dead, Eleanor is the object of Jack's passion; Candy and Marlis have each other—Candy having helped deliver Marlis's baby in the absence of Jack, and the two are together as lovers in the back seat of the Explorer during the storm. Never really divorced, Dot's "first love" (98) is Gerry, but he is gone, or appears only periodically; in *Tales* he is the hitchhiker who joins the four women in the red Explorer where, "alive in the wrecked cold" after surviving a plane crash, he appears to "seal her mouth with his" (374).

Such moments, though, are rare for Dot. More significant is that she capitalizes on her distance from Jack. In her alienated state, Hester cultivates a special knowledge of "the hidden sins" in others, the "unsunned snow" that contrasts with her own "burning shame" (61). Dot does something equivalent. Unlike the intuitive Hester, she is aggressive, inquisitive and brash, but this is her way of exposing others. Initially, she gets Jack to admit that she is "the goddamn fifth" of his wives, and almost stabs him with her knitting needle. "I don't know you from shit" (76–77), she says, while exposing his secret past with Eleanor. Often the mouthpiece of Erdrich's "pungent and smart" dialogue (Rev. of *Tales of Burning Love*, *Publishers Weekly*), Dot abhors superficial talk. At the funeral when Eleanor says Candace looks happy, Dot (a former classmate of Candy's) replies, "Scum floats" (129). Finally, it is Dot who sets the rules for each wife to tell her tale while the group is marooned in the North Fargo blizzard. The least romantic of the wives, Dot is the firebird who sets ablaze the others' secret lives.

Though fond of Jack, Dot finally sees him as her "burnt hope" (416), which is Hester's ultimate view of Dimmesdale. Recovering in the hospital after the storm, it is her mother Celestine, not Jack, who comes to her side. Erdrich seems to use Dot to assert, not sex or romance, but the extended family, so important to Native Americans. "Solid, responsible...brusque" (Childress), Dot's reserves her most genuine affection for Gerry, and a big priority in her life is to raise Shawn, whom she views as simply "my part of the deal" (417). Real life, after the romance is over, is Dot Nanapush's role, much as it finally becomes Hester Prynne's, who continues to mother Pearl while serving others after her lover is gone.

Five "Faces" in Review

So that is Erdrich's story—the five faces of Hester, so to speak, as reflected in the five wives of Jack Mauser. If Hester has a past marriage that has failed, causing her to flee across the sea, that is June Morrissey setting out in the snow near Williston in 1981. If Hester has had a secret life, where the passionate and sexual are intertwined with the spiritual and the saintly, that is Eleanor as she works out her relation to Jack in the convent garden in Argus in 1996, and later (after a vision of Leopolda) in a telling scene on the stairs with Jack to end the book. If Hester errs by allowing her former husband, now in America, to torture her new lover to the point of death, that is Candace, who is not able to sustain her relationship with Jack because he physically abuses her Pepperboy. If Hester needs to speak directly to her beloved and so takes him to the woods, where her words temporarily free the man from his rigidities, that is Marlis who ties up Jack and literally shows him what it feels like to be a woman. Finally, if Hester must still maintain a public face, in spite of all her inner worlds, that is Dot, the "live-in accountant" (70) of Jack Mauser, for whom personal love is not so important as the daily companionship of a man, the love of her family, and the knowledge that she can make things work.

Love's Added Dimension

There is an irony in *Tales* that may also be a modern comment on *The Scarlet Letter*, as Erdrich like Hawthorne focuses on her favorite themes, "the salvation of love" through "the power of narrative" (Ott). In *Tales*, two of the women, Candy and Marlis, struggle with each other. Candy, who would like a child, fawns on Marlis's baby—the baby she cannot have. If Jack has a problem with the pregnancy, Candy calls it "a treasure" (342), and it is she, not Jack, who helps in the delivery room. Though at first Marlis resists Candy's concern and affection, eventually their struggle—an important factor in both Hawthorne and Erdrich—brings them together where their "first kiss tells everything" (359). Finally, in the back of the Explorer in the snowstorm, they make love, having come to understand and accept each other as women—something Jack cannot seem to accomplish. This love affair serves as a foil for Hawthorne's portrayal of the relationship of Chillingworth and Dimmesdale—a story of revenge, hatred, and manipulation that destroys both men. It involves a different type of dispute, but the implication is that men have to control, while women's struggles lead to self-sacrifice and love. It is another kind of tale of burning love—sinful and scandalous, perhaps, in the eyes of many, but also respectful and caring, much like that between Hester and Dimmesdale in *The Scarlet Letter*.

The Scarlet Letter is a romantic novel that represents a landmark in the history of psychological love. Though deprecated by Hawthorne's critics at the time, the novel made a much deeper impression than his other works (Faust 140). One of the reasons, says Cotton, is that "the symbolic" is different from "the real" (57). Hester may have violated the Seventh Commandment, but she emerges as a free spirit who has integrated her sexual life into her being, and now, Dimmesdale notwithstanding, lives a rather Christ-like life in public. She has faults, however, as does he, and because of this, the story is tragic—a conflict between religion and its view of sexuality (Stubbs 85). What lives on in the reader, however, is a less-than-rigid notion of sexual love and its relation to holiness. Baym says that society's coming to love Hester shows its willingness to "make room for the human heart and its private needs" (58). Sandeen claims that in her public life she "bears the burden of man's affective nature, including outlawed passion," which the Puritan society tries to suppress "but cannot do without" (427). For these critics, *The Scarlet Letter* is, above all, a love story wherein the heroine transcends her culture.

Jack as Trickster

In *Tales of Burning Love*, Louise Erdrich uses *The Scarlet Letter* mythologically to paint a rather complex picture of love in a contemporary era. Jack Mauser may be a flawed human being; toward the end he is still dealing with Lyman Lamartine, the money-driven entrepreneur "planning for a casino" (406) whose devious ways are developed in *The Bingo Palace*. However, Jack is convincing as a modern male, a "satisfying multi-dimensional character" (Rifkind). A less-than-successful engineer, he is greedy, he drinks too much, he is ego-centered, but he likes and needs women in many ways. June is a fellow mixed-blood Chippewa with whom, even in her fragmented life, he momentarily identifies and ever after pursues her spirit. Dot, too, is connected to the reservation, a steady companion more than a lover, but still there, a crucial part of his work-a-day life. Jack's abusive side surfaces in his relationship with Candy, and it takes Marlis to teach him something about feeling with a woman. It may be in response to her that he ultimately comes to appreciate other human beings—their son, his own mother, all his wives.

Jack and Eleanor as Lovers

In the end, however, Eleanor is his real Hester Prynne, the one for whom his passion for life burns, and through whom it is finally satisfied. Lee says she represents "the passionate reversal" of his "sexual failure" with June. In contrast to Hawthrone, Erdrich makes sexuality, religion, and nature work together, so the ending is not tragic. Early on, Eleanor says, "Her love for Jack was still alive, disguised as everything. It ached pulled from the ground, it drew the air for her chest (83).

Later, in contrast to *The Scarlet Letter* where Hester departs for the forest after her lover's death, Erdrich in *Tales* actually brings "the forest" to bear on Eleanor and Jack; they consummate their love at the top of a staircase while outside "spears of grass rustled in their sheaths" (452). If Erdrich is a "master of the heightened intimate moment" (Harlan), it comes through such lyrical passages.

One of those coincidences in the novel that perhaps "stretch credulity" (Rifkind) is a miracle that sets up the finale—a phenomenon, says Max, Erdrich is "not afraid of involving" in her plots (116). Having survived the falling statue of a "stone woman"—a mysterious event testifying to the sainthood of Eleanor's idol, Sister Leopolda—we are told how exuberant he felt (441). So both Jack and Eleanor experience epiphanies that change their lives and bring them together sexually, with the stairs adding spiritual significance to their passion. Moreover, says Lee, the images surrounding the encounter suggest a Chippewa-like identification with the earth that Jack had suppressed (30).

Conclusion: The Other Face of Tragedy

That may be, but the seasons, too, are ever changing and unpredictable. Jack is still a modern male, a businessman, "charming, preening," and "self-destructive" (Rev. of *Tales of Burning Love*, *Publishers Weekly*). None of these women satisfy him completely, nor does he them. Eleanor says at one time that maybe "we each married a different man," as though it is Jack who has the different selves. Sister Leopolda tells Eleanor in her vision, "You and your sisters are blind women touching the vast body of the elephant..." (370). If that is so, then, it may be that any one woman, given her needs, must go through five individuals to find one good man. In *The Scarlet Letter*, Hester's love remains tragically unfulfilled, though symbolically she transcends her loss. Erdrich's love story ends with Eleanor's passionate fulfillment. Even so, it borders on tragedy that her counterparts must find other ways to keep the fire of love burning in a contemporary world less Puritan but more complex than Hawthorne had ever imagined.

Works Cited

Baym, Nina. "The Significance of Plot in Hawthorne's Romances."*Ruined Eden of the Present*. Ed. G. R. Thompson and Virgil L. Lokke. W. Lafayette: Purdue U P, 1981. 49–70.

Carpenter, Frederic I. "Scarlet A Minus." *College English* 5 (1944): 173–80.

Childress, Mark. "A Gathering of Widows." Rev. of *Tales of Burning Love*, by Louise Erdrich. *New York Review of Books* 12 May 1996: 10.

Cotton, Daniel. "Hawthorne versus Hester: The Ghostly Dialectic of Romance in *The Scarlet Letter*." *Texas Studies in Literature and Language* 24.1 (1982): 47–67.

Crews, Frederick C. "The Ruined Wall." *The Sins of the Fathers: Hawthorne's Psychological Themes* New York: Oxford U P, 1966. 136–53.

Curwen, Thomas. Rev. of *Tales of Burning Love,* by Louise Erdrich. *People Weekly* 27 May 1996: 38–39.

Erdrich, Louise. *The Beet Queen*. New York: Henry Holt, 1986.

Erdrich, Louise. *The Bingo Palace*. New York: HarperCollins, 1994.

Erdrich, Louise. *Love Medicine*. New York: Holt, Rinehart & Winston, 1984.

Erdrich, Louise. *Tales of Burning Love*. New York: HarperCollins, 1996.

Erdrich, Louise. *Tracks*. New York: Harper & Row, 1988.

Faust, Bertha. *Hawthorne's Contemporaneous Reputation*. New York: Octagon Books, 1968.

Fogel, Richard Harter. *Hawthorne's Imagery*. Norman: U of Oklahoma P, 1969.

Harlan, Megan. Rev. of *Tales of Burning Love*, by Louise Erdrich. *Entertainment Weekly* 17 May 1996: 57.

Harris, Marcia. "The Scenery Is Familiar in Erdrich's *Tales of Burning Love*." *Grand Forks Herald* 15 June 1996: 1B.

Hawthorne, Nathaniel. *The Scarlet Letter*. Ed. Seymour Gross, Sculley Bradley, Richmond Croom Beatty, and E. Hudson Long. 3rd ed. New York: W. W. Norton, 1988.

Hoffert, Barbara. Rev. of *Tales of Burning Love*, by Louise Erdrich. *Library Journal* 15 April 1996: 121.

Lee, Michael. "Erdrich's Dakota as Metaphor for American Culture." *National Catholic Reporter* 24 May 1996: 21, 30.

Max, D. T. "Prairie Fire." Rev. of *Tales of Burning Love*, by Louise Erdrich. *Harper's Bazaar* April 1996: 116–17.

Melville, Herman. *Moby Dick*. New York: Dell, 1959.

Ott, Bill. Rev. of *Tales of Burning Love*, by Louise Erdrich. *Booklist* 92.13 (1996): 1075.

Rev. of *Tales of Burning Love*, by Louise Erdrich. *Publishers Weekly* 19 February 1990: 202.

Rifkind, Donna. "Stories for a Stormy Night." Rev. of *Tales of Burning*

Love, by Louise Erdrich. *Wall Street Journal* 24 April 1996: A12.

Sandeen, Ernest. "*The Scarlet Letter* as a Love Story." *PMLA* 77 (1962): 425–35.

Stubbs, John Caldwell. "*The Scarlet Letter*: 'A Tale of Human Frailty and Sorrow.'" *The Pursuit of Form: A Study of Hawthorne and the Romance* Urbana: U of Illinois P, 1970. 81–102.

Tan, Amy. "The Many Voices of America." *Westminster Town Hall Forum.* NPR. KCCD, Moorhead, 22 Sept. 1994.

Wood, Dave. "The Book Queen." Interview with Louise Erdrich. *Minneapolis Star Tribune* 15 April 1996: E1, E2.

Contributors

Jeane C. Breinig is currently Assistant Professor of English at the University of Alaska Anchorage. She is Haida and of the Taaslaanas Brown Bear Clan, raised in Kasaan and Ketchikan Alaska.

Heatherly Brooke Bucher, of mixed Cherokee and European heritage, received a B.A. in English from Oklahoma Baptist University and has since presented papers at various conferences, including the 20th Century Literature Conference and the American Culture Association Conference.

Blanca Chester received her Ph.D. from the Programme of Comparative Literature at the University of British Columbia. Her interests include Native American literatures and the study of Native American and First Nations oral traditions. She has worked extensively with ethnographer Wendy Wickwire on the translation of Okanagan storyteller, Harry Robinson's, narratives from oral into written forms. Her dissertation is entitled, "Narrativity and Orality in the Native American Novel: Genres of Representation." She is currently teaching at Simon Fraser University in British Columbia.

Maurice Collins received his B.A. from Boston College and his M.A. and Ph.D. from Brown University, and currently lives in Providence, RI.

John K. Donaldson is an Associate Professor at George Washington University in Washington, D.C., where he teaches courses in ethnohistory, Native North American peoples and cultures, American culture through film, and English language. He holds Master's degrees in literature and in linguistics and a doctorate in American civilization with a specialization in ethnohistory (Native American history). He is the author of *The Native Americans*, a U.S. government (Division for the Study of the United States) publication.

Carrie Etter is presently a doctoral candidate in English at the University of California, Irvine. She has published essays and reviews on many contemporary poets, and her poems have appeared in *Arshile, Seneca Review, Poetry Wales*, and *The Anthology of Magazine Verse and Yearbook of American Poetry 1995–96*.

Sidner Larson (Gros Ventre) is Director of the Native Studies Program at Iowa State University. He is author of the autobiographical *Catch Colt* (University of Nebraska Press) and of *Captured in the Middle: Tradition and Experience in Contemporary Native American Writing* (University of Washington Press).

Tom Matchie is Professor of English at North Dakota State University. He has written and published extensively on American Indian subjects, particularly on Louise Erdrich.

Elizabeth Hoffman Nelson is a lecturer in English at the State University of New York, College at Fredonia. She is Co-editor of Peter Lang's *American Indian Studies Series*, and serves as chair for the American Culture Association's American Indian Literatures and Cultures area. Her most recent publication was in *Leslie Marmon Silko: A Collection of Critical Essays* (University of New Mexico Press, 1999).

Malcolm A. Nelson is Distinguished Teaching Professor of English at the State University of New York, College at Fredonia. He is a Co-editor of Peter Lang Publishing's *American Indian Studies Series*. He has published widely on Mari Sandoz, Robin Hood, Catches and Glees, and American burying grounds.

Robert M. Nelson is a Professor of English at the University of Richmond, where since 1975 he has taught courses in twentieth-century American literature and, since 1988, American Indian literatures. From 1989 until 1997 he served as Production Editor for the journal *Studies in American Indian Literatures*. He is the author of *Place and Vision: The Function of Landscape in Native American Fiction* (Peter Lang, 1993).

Conrad Shumaker is originally from Tucson, Arizona, and he now teaches in the English Department at the University of Central Arkansas. His essays have appeared in such journals as *American Literature*, *The Arizona Quarterly*, and *The Journal of American Culture*. He would like to thank Patricia Washington McGraw for her creative partnership in developing the course from which this essay arose.

Scott Manning Stevens (Karoniaktatie), a member of the St. Regis Mohawk Tribe, received his B.A. from Dartmouth College and his M.A. and Ph.D. from Harvard University. Scott is currently an Assistant Professor of English and American Indian Studies at Arizona State University. There he teaches various courses in Renaissance and early modern literatures, including the literature of the Age of the Encounter. He has published essays on early modern science and the body and on the construction of Native American ethnic identities in early American literature. Scott is currently the Editor of *ASAIL Notes*, the quarterly news letter for the Association for Study of American Indian Literatures.

Jeri Zulli is a graduate student and instructor in American Literature in the English Department at The George Washington University in Washington, D.C. Additionally, she is an adjunct professor and Director of the Writing Center at the Wesley Theological Seminary in Washington.

Index